When My Soul Cried

Natoshia E. Mitchell

Introduction

"In the Midst of it All"

My testimony is an example of healing, forgiveness and deliverance. No matter where you are in life or where you've been, God can and will heal you! There is no problem too big or too small for him to handle. God states in his word, "He will never leave you nor forsake you, Hebrew 13: 5-6 NIV." I have gone through many trials, tribulations and tests at one point in life I felt like Job. I thought I was going to lose my mind, I felt I was so low there was no way God could pick me up. I thought after all the things I had gone through. God would not forgive me but he changed me and has forgiven me for all my sins (Psalms 103 NIV).

This is based on my encounters with the Holy Spirit, getting saved, people I trusted talking about me, being in an abusive relationship, my dreams, my ungodly soul ties with men, as well as friends, the lost of my two children Antonio De'Shawn Brazel and A'miya Janea Mitchell, and finally being delivered and set free from the hands of the enemy.

I don't know where to begin when I say God has been truly good to me. Through everything; he has bestowed grace and mercy upon me and provided protection over my life. There were times I should have been in jail, in my grave, or in a mental hospital, but God still had his hands on my life, sustained my mind, and spared me from the traps of the enemy. I am eternally grateful.

Acknowledgements

First, I would like to give all my thanks to who is first in my life, my first love, my *Lord and Savior Jesus Christ*. Without him it would not be possible to deliver my testimony to you. From my heart to yours, God is in the midst of all blessings.

To my grandparents Deacon E. Mells and Sister L. Mells, who instilled wisdom and introduced me to the Lord. My grandma was a virtuous woman and granddaddy showed me how a real man is supposed to treat a woman. Grandma, you taught me everything about being a woman of wisdom. You took my brother and me in when no one wanted us, and you defended us when others talked about us and said, "We would be nothing or never amount to anything." Thank you... *Look at me now!*

To my mother Liz L. Mells II, even though it was a rough start in our journey as mother and daughter; you taught me survival skills of life, you taught me how to make a dollar out of fifteen cents, and you always told me "A wise head carries a still tongue." I never knew what it meant until I became older and had to face "life" itself. You taught me to hold my head up high no matter what people say; because the same ones talking and throwing stones are the same ones that have more skeletons in their closets. You stood by me when I had my son at a young age and for that I say *"Thank you Mommy, I love you so much."*

To my two beautiful children O'neisha K. Sermon (Nique), An'treyon O. Sermon (Trey) and my grandbaby "A'mia K. Ogbeka (Mimi), I love you with everything in me (all my heart). You are the best gifts any mother could ask for, you are my joy, and you lift my spirit every morning we wake up in prayer together. You make my life worth living, and I give God the praise for blessing me with two beautiful children.

To my sisters Shakita L. Tensley and Ashley V. Tensley, thank you for giving me the opportunity to be a mother as well as your big sister. Although we have had our ups and downs like sisters do, we always manage to stick together no matter what. Remember when we would stay up late nights laughing and imitating people? Shakita, I promise I will never play circus with you again. You are not only my little sisters but you are also my children, and I love you so much more than you will ever know.

My sister Tenisha Mitchell my prayer warrior, the day you came into my life, I did not just gain a sister I was blessed with a best friend. We talk about everything, laugh, cry. I am beyond grateful God connected us. I Love you.

To Stanley T. Mitchell, even though you're gone to be with the Lord. Thank you for always protecting me, giving me wisdom about men and standing up for me all the time. Our love is so strong; it's hard to face the fact that you are gone. But knowing you gave your life to the Lord gives me so much peace and joy. I miss you so much, and I know you are watching over me.

To Deborah R. Mells, where do I begin? It has been an honor and a blessing to have you in my life. Thank you Auntie for *always* being there for me no matter what; you spent time with me on the weekends and straightened my hair "Even though sometimes you burned me" you never listened to what anyone said about Liz's kid's, and you never let it stop your love for my brother and me. It means a lot to me to know you cared so much. You protected us when our mother would beat on us; you and Uncle Buddy were the only ones that would come to our rescue. We would be up for hours at night talking, crying and laughing. You always taught me the importance of going to college, life and having a career. I admire you so much; even though you are my aunt I feel like you are a second mother to me. I love you so much; I give God thanks he placed you in our lives.

To my aunts Thelma and Willie Mae thank you for your all your prayers and being there for me every time I needed you spiritually and financially, thank you for helping me with my sisters after the passing of my mother. I love you

To Tammy Rolle, thank you for your spiritual emails, encouraging words, your push and believing in me about owning my own business. You will always have a big place in my heart. I have so much love for everyone in so many different ways. I just want to thank everyone for being in my life. I am very grateful to have every one of you in my life and you are very important to me. My soul is touched; my heart and spirit are forever blessed. It is the little things that count.

Most of all I would like to thank the individuals who treated me wrong, because you pushed me into my destiny and prosperity. The evil words you spoke over my life no longer penetrate my spirit. The things you said I would never be, I masticated up and spit out. And God has turned the names you called me into a song of beauty. What you meant for harm, God turned it around for the good, blessed me and my family, and now I am truly a testimony! Love always, Natoshia

Table of Contents

Tested with Tithe

See My Change

Struggle to Breathe

Behind the Fist

Murder by Man

Extraordinary Woman

Building Comprehensive Solution to Domestic Violence

(Six weeks to rebuilding and reshaping your life)

Week 1   "Breaking the Cycle"

Week 2   "Healing"

Week3   "Forgiveness"

Week 4   "Finding Your Purpose"

Week 5   "Loving Yourself"

Week6   "New Beginnings"

Psalms 23 (NIV) "My Rock"

The Lord is my shepherd; I shall not want.

He maketh me to lie down in green pastures; He leadeth me beside the still waters. He

restored my soul; he leadeth me in the path of righteousness for his name sake.

Yea, though I walk through the valley of the shadows of death,

I will fear no evil: for thou art with me; thy rod the staff the comfort me.

Thou prepare a table before me in the presence of mine enemies: He anoints my head with oil;

my cup runs over.

Surely goodness and mercy shall follow me for all the days of my life and

I will dwell in the house of the Lord forever. Amen

Matthew 6:9-13 (NIV)

"My Strength and my Everything"

Our Father, who art in heaven, Hallowed would be thy name. Thy kingdom come, thy

will be done, on earth as it is in heaven.

Give us this day our daily bread. And forgive us our debts, as we forgive our debtors.

Lead us not into temptation, but deliver us from evil. For thine is the kingdom, the

power and the glory. Forever and ever

In Jesus name........Amen

My Diary

My Story

My Testimony

My Glory

My Deliverance

"The Woman in the Mirror"

As I looked in the mirror, I was staring at a woman with a lot of pain, so much pain that joy and peace were far from me. I was staring at woman buried in bondage abused from childhood and adulthood. The woman in the mirror did not know who she was. In fact her soul was lost, and she was living in grief and anger from her past, which had created an unknown character. From the outside, you would never know her pain because she kept herself looking like a diva. But inside her body was full of pain and tears from crying at night; sometimes even during the day.

One day I looked in the mirror after having a long a talk with God, I didn't know who the woman was looking back at me. I never realized it was my own testimony staring back at me, a reflection of who I had become. As I continued to look in the mirror, I realized I was looking at one of God's creations. A woman! The beginning! The change! The shift! The one God called to heal other women who have been or still in abusive relationships, or families that have lost children as the result of death.

My past is my past (it's history); my future is my gift from God.

The woman in the mirror knew she was more than just a booty call, but tall, thick men had always been her weakness. She knew she was better than being second choice in a man's life and she knew life was more than just sex. But for some reason she didn't care. She felt having a piece of a man was better than having no man at all! The woman in the mirror is a mother, a sister, a friend, an aunt, a nurse, a teacher, a mother and father to her children. The woman in the mirror sometimes lost herself in the midst of it all....

After going out to different clubs with my best friend and partying every weekend, I had always felt it was something inside of me that was missing, something I couldn't explain. Going to the clubs, I never felt comfortable I just went, it was away to escape everything for the moment. My wounds were so deep, only God could heal. My heart was like a broken glass, but I didn't know where to find the main piece to begin to put it all back together. I visited many churches searching to be delivered and set free, but found myself still lost in this world. I felt as though I was sentenced to life without a trial.

One night I went to a revival with my aunt. I walked in and sat down with my kids, thinking to myself, "This is not going to work; I don't know why I am here." But my aunt said, "You need to be in this revival, God has a word for you." While I was in service, the Prophetess kept staring at me. Occasionally I would look back at her. I wonder what she was looking at. After the praise and worship, the Prophetess began her sermon. The anointing was flowing so heavily, it felt as though I was at the feet of Jesus. She called me to the front. I was scared to go up, my hand was wet from sweat, and I didn't know what she was going to say to me. She began to prophesy to me, and she was on point with a lot of things. I said to myself," How in the world does this woman know about me?" After she gave her testimony about herself, I said softly, "Our lives are somewhat the same." After she prayed for me and ministered to my spirit, my life has never been the same. And at that moment, I was delivered and set free from past relationships. Although I was delivered from a lot of things, the wounded little girl was still holding on inside. I cried for weeks after services because I could still feel the presence and the anointing of God on my life. The service was powerful; she understood me and everything I was going through. I had never met her before and God had used her to deliver me from what I needed to take me to the next level. Prophetess Sims never judged me. When I was going through deliverance, she held my hands, and we went through together.

The woman in the mirror knows how to allow God to stretch her child support $13.29, a year later less than $200 for two children (at times the state only send the check when they felt like sending it to me). When the woman in the mirror requested a modification for an increase in child support, the father denied the increase to make it hard for her. The woman in the mirror still held down a steady job and pursued her college degree without depending on the father of her children for help. However, on March 18, 2011 her child support increased to $520, still not enough for two children but to God be the glory. The woman in the mirror gave God the biggest praise!

The woman in the mirror recognizes when the enemy is attacking. She knows how to seek strong prayer warriors God has placed in her life. In the midst of it all, she knows how to hold her head up high and be a better person. The woman in the mirror survivor the death of two children by the age of twenty-seven years old, her son was murdered and daughter never given a chance at life. She survived the burying of her daughter while the father, a sergeant in the United States Army, chose not to attend the funeral or even acknowledge he had a daughter. Years later he sent an email apologizing for his absence in A'miya's life and for not being there when she passed away. The woman in the mirror returned the e-mailed letting him know she had forgiven him a long time ago. The woman in the mirror son Antonio was murdered at the age of two years old. She lost both parents at the age of forty-eight, two weeks apart, and lost both of her brothers. She was in an abusive relationship, and brokenhearted but held on to her mind because God would not allow the enemy to steal it. Although she is a go-getter and soul searcher, she knew her strength would come from God in the *midst of it all.*

The woman in the mirror is at a revival, when her two sisters ran into the church screaming, "Mom is dead!" She ran out of the church, when she arrives at the located her Mother's body was laying on the floor. The paramedic's trying to resuscitate her, but she was pronounced dead at the scene. The woman in the mirror grabs her two sisters, get in her car and follow the Paramedic's to the hospital. She looked at her Mother laying in the hospital bed, while the tears roll down her face asking God, "Why?"

The woman in the mirror went into the funeral home while her mother lay on a table. She held Peaches's hand as they both approached the table slowly towards her mother. She did her mother's make up, Peaches did her hair, and they both dressed her together. Peaches polished her nails; we made sure that my mother's last appearance was the best. Two weeks later after work, while getting dinner ready for my two younger sisters and her two younger children, the phone rang. The woman in the mirror just received news her father was killed in an automobile accident; he died instantly.

Now the woman in the mirror has to continue to raise her two younger sisters because, three months prior to their parent's death, her brother was shot seven times (he survived) but he needed physical therapy. The woman in the mirror is still holding on to God's word; she knows her faith is her strength. She remembers Job losing it all then God blessing him with everything and even more. God said in his word, "He will never leave you nor forsake you, (Hebrews 13:5 NIV)." The woman in the mirror knows that God has a purpose in her life; she knows this too shall pass.

Now

God has blessed the woman in the mirror with two beautiful children and a granddaughter. The woman in the mirror received her Bachelors', MBA and now pursing her Doctorate degree. The woman in the mirror knows how to stop and allow God to move in her life; she knows the intimacy of God (it's a beautiful thing). She knows how to step back one step, so God can make two steps for her path. She understands that "No weapon formed against her shall prosper and every tongue that rises against her shall be condemned (Isaiah 54:17)." The woman in the mirror knows the favor of God and the blessing of Abraham is on her life and her generation to come.

Who is that woman in the mirror?

The woman in the mirror is ME........

Bad Relationships

There comes a point in our lives when that divine woman inside of us has to come out, stand her ground, and be the woman God designed her to be. It doesn't matter how many mistakes you have made or what you have done, God will forgive you according to Psalms chapter 103. Yes, sometimes it is hard to stay focused when going through trials, and sometimes in the midst of it all, we become mad at the world or even mad at God. But knowing God will never leave us nor forsake us is the start of our healing process.

Sometimes as a woman we confuse lust with real love and don't pay enough attention to the signs. We sometimes look at every relationship as "This could be the right one" settle down too quickly, making him a priority and being an option or choice between other women. We ignore the fact that we may not be the only woman in his lives.

I did not have my father in my life, so knowing true love from a man was not a choice for me. Granddaddy tried to do the best, but like he always said, "Men these days are not the same when I was coming up." I am not saying all men are out to hurt women; as women we sometimes go through enough hurt and we cannot see when God has really sent our husbands. We are so confused and many times fighting with other women, even to the point of making fools out of ourselves in public. We ignore the fact that they have bad credit, too many baby mommas', and a crazy baby momma who can't get over them and want to cause strife. We ignore the fact they are behind in child support, drug dealers, have no job, live in the clubs looking for their next victim. The only time they step foot in a church; is for weddings or funerals, and they both involve food and alcohol.

We as women have become stuck or involved in bad relationships because, somewhere along the way, we have allowed Satan to steal our identity, our destiny, and our purpose in life. We allow our past to control our future, and most of all, who we are as Christians. The one thing I have learned through bad relationships is," If a man doesn't fear God; you are dealing with a dangerous man, (Proverbs 3:7, 28; 14 NIV)." I have learned to sit back and wait on God because the man I was choosing as a king over my life and my children was not in God's plan for us. The man that God has for you will not come with a line he rehearsed with his homeboys. You will not have to tell him what you are looking for in a man he will already know because God will have already revealed it to him; he will know you by your fruit.

Lack of Knowledge

Being a woman is more than just opening your legs to a man that has no intention of being your husband. Before a man approaches you he has already decided among his friends and sometimes made an agreement with the devil, where you stand in his life. The man that God has for you will know that God has a covenant over you and will make you his wife.

As women, we make the mistake of thinking we can control a man with sexually pleasures. In reality it's almost impossible to control a man, with many options available to them; it's up to us as women to pray for the gift of discernment, protection, wisdom, directions, and guidance. With the power of prayer you will know what type of man he is before he even opens his mouth (*You have the power to stop the devil in his tracks*).

Being a strong woman is not just about making your money or laying on your back with the bottom of your feet facing God. It's about getting to know the real intimacy of God and his character. It's about developing a relationship with God, loving herself, knowing who you are as a woman, furthering your education, and being a role model for your children. There's nothing sharper than a woman who can walk on a job backed up with a degree and still come home and be a virtuous woman. If you can wait a little longer and trust God, your husband will find you.

There are some men in our past we will look back on and ask, "What was I thinking?" If he can't wait it means, he has no relationship with God (which is dangerous), he will not respect you, and he has only one thing on his mind. Save yourself from disappointments and heartaches, and wait on God. You will be glad you did.

What is a Woman's Worth If She Loses Her Soul?

How Do You Heal When Hurt Is Everywhere You Turn?

Sometimes hurt is God's way of getting your attention. Think about it; when you can't sleep at night God wants to talk to you, he wants to hear from you, when someone cheats on you or you lost your job. God wants you to put your trust in him. God tries to get your attention for number of reasons. It depends on where you are in your life and where God wants to take you. For me, I prayed, "Lord please heal the wounds of the little girl inside and set her free, break every ungodly soul tie from every relationship (mentally, spiritually and sexually)" Deliver me for the spirit of girlfriend. I was tired of making the same mistakes over and over in my life, so I decided to get to the root of the problem. The little girl inside of me was still crying, and her heart was broken. She felt there was no end to being beaten down and broken. God heals the brokenhearted and binds up their wounds (Psalms 147:3 NIV). O LORD my God, I cried out to you, and you healed me (Psalms 30:2, NIV).

When I said those prayers, I was in my room, I had just moved in my apartment in New Tampa and I told my kids, "If no one is dying or bleeding, do not knock on my door!" I closed the door and I cried out to God for hours. I mean seriously crying out to God. I prayed so hard I could hardly breathe from crying so much. I began to feel something pulling from me. It felt heavy, and as I opened my eyes I could see a little girl fighting to come back to me. I began to pray even harder until she disappeared. I felt weak afterward; I just laid there rejoicing in the presence of the Lord. I was set free from bondage of my childhood; the wounded little girl that was trapped within was gone. It felt good; I felt light. I don't know how long I was in my room, because I lost track of time. When I opened the door, my kids were sound asleep, and I began kissing on them, and praising God even more.

My healing began when I went to the enemy camp and took back what the devil had stolen from me. I had finally faced what I was running from. I had made up in my mind, I wasn't running anymore. I have God on my side, and I know the power of prayer changes things.

In the Midst

I was born September 4. My parents were Darrell Mitchell and Liz Mells II. Both of them were high school sweetheart and graduated from the same high school in St. Petersburg, Florida. After being off and on in a relationship with my father, my mother went to live with my grandparents shortly after I was born. Although my mother and father weren't on the best of terms, she still tried to keep it together. No matter what was going in her life the world never knew it. Unfortunately, because my dad loved more women then he could handle, my mom became a single parent. My mother always told me because I was her first born she did not have a full understanding of being a parent. So finally my grandmother told my mother," Give me Toshia and get your life together. I will take care of her." My mother was very pleased with the decision because she felt it was a new beginning for her. She then began to travel a lot; I remember her going to live in Detroit, Michigan and went to Chicago with her best friend. As I got order I realized my mother was running from pain. Maybe she was running from the little girl inside of her.

As time went on, my mother would come get me on the weekends. She tried to be the best mother she could be. A few years later, my mother got pregnant again, with my brother Stanley, who was born on February 21, and that's when my life changed. She became a single parent of two. I know some people ask, "You were two years old; how would you know?" When pain begins, it doesn't matter how old you are. You will never forget it, and at some point in your life, something will trigger your memory.

My mother always felt others looked at her as the black sheep in the family because she spoke her mind. She did not hold back on her feelings, and you knew if she liked you or not. I would say she wasn't phony, unlike most people I have known in my lifetime. I grew up on 21st and Queensboro Avenue in St. Petersburg, Florida, It wasn't the best neighborhood, but it wasn't the worst, either. I had many friends, and we always had fun. I can really say living on Queensboro Avenue was like living around family.

My grandfather was a deacon, and my grandmother was a deaconess. We attended services almost every night of the week, so at a very young age, my brother and I knew about every meeting held in the church. When I was young, my brother and I would be sitting on the front row and fall asleep during services. He would be laying one way and I would be laying the other way.

As we became older, my mother grew very irritated with everything we did as children. She became frustrated due to the lack of support from my father and not receiving any child support. She began to beat us with whatever she could get her hands on (cords, brooms, and her fist). What could I do, except pray as Grandma taught me. Some family members weren't any help; they would pick on my brother and me saying, "You'd better go, before Liz comes and mold your head." I would shoot a bird and roll my eyes at them. As time went on hearing hurtful words became a buildup of anger and hate towards a lot of people.

One night I asked my Grandma, "Why don't people like us in the family and why don't they want us to play with their kids?" Grandma replied saying," Baby, you don't worry about what people say or do. You leave them in the hands of God; he will take care of them. You just wait and see. God will always make your enemies your footstool" I looked at her and smiled. Grandma always had a way of making my brother and I feel at home and loved. She did not care about what other people said about Liz's kids. Grandma would say, "You are my baby and that's what matter, you be who you are and not what they say or think." Grandma's words to this day have gotten me through many rough times in my life. I reflect on them every time I am going through hard times. If it wasn't for God placing my Grandparents in my life, I don't know where I would be. Grandma was the best in this world. Until this day I have never meet a woman like her. She never cursed, drank or smoked, never talked bad about people or even raised her voice. She would feed and help anyone that came to her. Grandma always said," My blessings will come from God, and if I don't get them here on earth, I will get them when I enter the golden gates." Grandma always had such strong faith.

Suicide Attempted

I was around 11 years old, my brother and I were walking with my mother to her apartment. She had just finished arguing with Grandma, so I knew she was not in a good mood, and it was beat-down time at any given moment. I began to cry because I did not want to go. Tremyne (Stanley) looked at me and said, "You better stop crying before ma beat you!" I continued to cry because I did not want to leave Grandma. Grandma was upset, and she begged my momma not to take us. She told her to go home and calm down. When we got to her place, she said to me, "If you don't stop crying, I will knock you out!" I looked at her with fear, but I continued to cry. She beat me with her fist and pulled my hair, yelling, "Didn't I tell you to shut the hell up!" I could see chunks of my hair on the floor. My brother began to cry and I broke loose from her and ran as fast as I could.

When I arrived at my Grandma's house, and I knocked as hard as I could, yelling, "Open the door!" The side of my face was swollen and I had scratches on the side of my face and neck. Grandma called my uncle. He came to the house and looked at the side of my face; he shook his head and looked down. Grandma said, "I don't know what to say about Liz; she don't have the sense God gave her!" Grandma rubbed her hands together when she was worried or upset. About thirty minutes later we heard a knock at the door; it was a police officer.

Grandma opened the door, and he said, "Is there a Natoshia here?" Her mother reported her as a runway." Grandma looked at the officer and said, "She is not a runway. You don't understand. This girl has been beaten by her mother, and if you take her back, she is going to beat her again for running." The officer stated, "Her mother reported her as a runway, and by state law, her mother is her legal guardian. We have to take her back home." I looked at the officer, Grandma and my uncle. I didn't want go back because I knew my mother was going to beat me for running away. As they were in the living room talking, trying to convince the officer not to take me back, I walked into the kitchen, and opened the cabinet where Grandma had her antique dish sets. She kept her all her medicine at the top of the shelf. I grabbed her bottle of sleeping pills and poured them all into my hands. I swallowed as many as I could, and by that time the officer saw me take my hand from my mouth and ran over to me. I could hear Grandma crying out to the Lord," Save my grandchild." My uncle was pacing back and forth. The police officer called the paramedic, when they arrived; EMT's started an IV in my arm. When I arrived at Bayview Medical Center, I was given thick, black, sweetish stuff; which made me throw up all the medication I had taken. The doctors evaluated me for a couple of hours before I was taken to a hospital for teens. When I arrived, I meet other teenagers who had tried to commit suicide as well. I was in the hospital for seventy-two hours before the judge released me to my grandma. I felt empty, as though everyone in the world was gone, and I was the only one left in it. When I received counseling, I felt it really didn't help, I wondered can a counselor help me if that person had never been abused.

One night a girl came up to me and said, "Stop crying; if you continue to cry, they will not let you go home. The doctors will think you are still depressed. When you talk to the nurse or doctor, talk with confidence, and don't sound like you are depressed or sad." I listened to her because she had done the same thing and was being released. I didn't realize I had learned how to cover my true feelings, how to pretend everything is okay. "But all I could think about was sad things like, how my brother and I were in a foster home because my mother went to jail. She and was facing fifteen years for fighting over my dad. Nobody else came but Grandma and Granddaddy. My brother and I were playing in the background on the swing set, and that's when I saw the face of my Grandparents.

I felt so much darkness around me, even at a young age. Although my Grandparents were a big part of our lives, it's not the same when you don't have your mother and father to fill that parental void. It's like something is missing in your life and you cannot explain what it is.

After being in the hospital for seventy-two hours, my Grandma and my aunt picked me up, Grandma took me home. When I got home, she said, "Go take a bath. You were surrounded by so many different spirits, you must bathe, and I am going to pray over you when you get out." I looked at her with tears in my eyes and I said Grandma," I don't know what else to do, she will not stop beating us, why is she so mad? What am I doing so wrong? Am I worth saving?" My grandma held me in her bosom, took a deep breath, and said, "Grandma is here, and everything is going to be alright; don't you worry." The following weekend my Aunt Deborah came and got me. When my mother tried to come and see me, my aunt said to her, "You are at my house now; you play by my rules, and you will not hit her around me." My momma said, "I don't want to hit her, I just want to tell her I am sorry." My momma came into the room. I looked at her, and my aunt stood by the door. She grabbed me and said, "I am sorry!" And as her daughter, I forgave her, like I always did. My aunt Deborah kept me for that weekend; she did this a lot.

The next morning Auntie Deborah got up, washed my hair and then she straightened it. I felt like a new person on the outside. She talked to me and told me, "Never accept when someone says you will never be anything in life. You are somebody, and I love you." Her words always stayed with me because she was the only person beside Grandma that never turned her back on me and my brother; Auntie Deborah was like a mother and friend to me. As the years continued my brother and I were still abused until we became of an age when we were able to defend ourselves. My brother and I always felt when we looked in certain family members' eyes; we could see how they continued to feel. It was like looking at hate through their soul. It was like we could hear them continue to say "They will never be anything" or "Those just Liz kids." Who cares! How you feel, or what you think does not define me as a woman, you no longer have control, and your words aren't insignificant.

Antonio

It was March 15, 1987, I was fourteen years old. I met and fell in love with a young man named Boris. We meet through my cousin Brandy, actually he is her cousin on her mother's side of the family, and I am her cousin on her father's side of the family. When I saw Boris I wondered, "Who is that?" At the time he was dating someone else. I didn't care; I was out to get him. I had my mind set on "What I want is what I will get." I felt he is not married and we are just fourteen years old.

Later that day I asked Brandy, "Who is that?"

She said, "Oh, that's my cousin Boris, he just moved here from New Jersey."

I said, "Oh really! Well, you tell him I like him." Brandy laughed and told him what I said.

Later that day I asked Grandma if I could spend the night with Brandy, grandma said, "Okay, let me talk to her mom and make sure she is going to be home." Grandma talked to her mom, and they agreed that it was okay for me to spend the night with Brandy. We stayed up all night talking about Boris.

We called him on the phone and talked all night. Boris and I began dating, and we fell in love with each other. I was his first love and he was mine. We talked on the phone all the time; he was different to me. I felt he was the sexiest young man in the world. He was tall, dark, sexy, handsome and most of all, he protected me like my brother did. That drew me closer to him, and as time went on, I asked my mother to put me on birth control pills. She looked at me and said, "What!" She hit me so hard, I fell to the floor. When I got up, I ran to Boris's grandma's house, where he was standing outside.

I told him what my momma had done. He was mad but there was nothing he could do about it. The next day we skipped school because we thought she was going to call the police again and tell them I ran away. I knew they were going to take me back to the fire furnace. I felt the law was not willing to protect or listen to me regarding my mother beating us. I felt the system failed me so many times that there was no need to look to them for protection.

Boris and I went to his father's house later that day. We talked about everything I was going through in my life. I was feeling at that moment I was put on this earth to suffer. He pulled me close to him, and he kissed me and one thing lead to another. We did things we had no business doing, but I felt comfort, and I didn't want to stop. I felt if I had a baby, I could get my own place, and I could protect myself from my mom. A few weeks later I became sick, and I didn't understand what was going on with my body. All I knew was I was in love. Boris understood me, and he was there to comfort me.

One day after school, I asked a friend to come with me to the clinic to take a pregnancy test, and she agreed. We went to the clinic, I took a pregnancy test, and sure enough it was positive. I was so scared I called Boris. He picked us up and I just handed him the paper. He looked at me with big eyes, but I could tell he was somewhat happy in a way, though scared. I asked him, "What are we going to do?" He said, "I don't know but you will not get rid of my child." I said, "Okay!" We dropped my friend off at home, went to his grandma's house, and told her I was pregnant. She began fussing at us, but the damage was already done. It was getting late, so I knew I had to make it home before it got dark.

Boris dropped me off around the corner from my grandma's house. I walked in the house with fear on my face; I just knew the Lord was going to tell Grandma I was pregnant. Grandma just had this way of knowing things, and she would always say, "The Lord will tell me." She had a faith and a relationship with God that was unexplainable. So I decided to wait and let the Lord tell her I was pregnant.

As time went on, I hid my pregnancy. I would buy tampons as if I were having my cycle every month. I went to church every Sunday, and sang in the choir. I did everything I would normally do; I hid my pregnancy for six months. I would tell Grandma I was going to a friend's house on Saturday mornings, and I would go to the doctor. My aunt tried to tell my grandma I was pregnant, but I denied it. There was no way in the world I was ready to face the disappointment and hurt Grandma was going to feel. No one was going to make me. I continued to deny I was pregnant.

One day I was lying on the floor. I had fallen asleep, and my shirt must have come up while I was asleep. Grandma woke me calling my name "Natoshia" I knew when she called my name like that, I was in trouble. When I woke up, she asked me, "Toshia are you pregnant?"

I said, "No!" Grandma said, "I am going to ask you again, if you lie, I am going to hit you so hard, you will think lighting struck you." Are you pregnant?"

I said, "Yes!" She hit me so hard I saw sparks of stars flashing before my eyes. I didn't know Grandma could hit so hard. Grandma had seen the dark line going down my stomach. She asked, "How far along are you?" I said, "Six months." Grandma looked at me with tears in her eyes, and I cried too. I fell to my knees saying, "Grandma, I'm so sorry!" Grandma was more upset that I went so long without telling her, but I had been scared she was going to make me get an abortion. Before I had gotten pregnant, and had to get an abortion. I wanted my child; I wanted to receive love back unconditionally.

Two months later on November 14, 1990, I was sitting home watching TV. I did not go to school that day because I had just left the hospital the previous night, and I was at risk for having an early labor. The doctor had told me to go home and get plenty of rest. As I was sitting down, my underwear was wet. I just thought it was the baby on my bladder. My cousin had her baby a few months earlier. I asked her, "What does it mean when your panties are wet?"

She said, "Girl, you might be in labor! If it happens again, let me see" I said, "Girl, I don't want you looking at my panties!"

She said, "You are so crazy! We are cousins, and I'm trying to see if you are in labor or not.

Oh! Crazy girl!"

We both started laughing and I said, "Okay!"

About thirty minutes later, it happened again, but this time it was a lot of fluid coming out. I looked at my cousin and said, "Girl! I don't know what this is but it just happened again, and this time it is a lot!"

So she and I went into the bathroom, and I showed her. She ran out of the bathroom yelling, "Grandma! Toshia is in labor, and her water just broke!"

Grandma said, "Oh Lord! Call your mother, she has my car. Auntie came and took me to the hospital. The pain began to increase, as tears rolled down my face. When I arrived at the hospital, I was rushed to the delivery room. Grandma looked and me and said, "Baby, I got to go. Call me when you have the baby. This is a pain grandma can't help you with, and I hate to see you in so much pain." I looked at her and said,

"Grandma I understand. It is okay." Grandma kissed me on my forehead, and auntie grabbed my hand. Auntie and Grandma left the hospital, and my cousin stayed with me.

She looked at me and asked, "You want me to go and get Boris?"

I said, "Yea; hurry up because I think this baby is coming soon!"

She said, "Okay!" About twenty minutes later Boris came running into the delivery room. He was smiling and kissing me all over my face.

I looked at him and said, "This is it. We are going to be parents soon."

He said, "I know!" About ten minutes later I told Boris, "I think I have to go to the restroom" He said, "Okay, let me help you."

A pain hit, and I laid back down. I told him, "Go, and get the nurse!" Boris ran out yelling, "Nurse, we need help!"

When the nurse came in, she said, "Oh my, I see the baby's head; don't push!" And forty-five minutes later I gave birth to our son; we named him Antonio De'Shawn Brazel; he was born a month early. He and weighed only 5 pounds 10 ½ ounces. Grandma was happy after Antonio was born, though she did not like the fact that his father had become one of the biggest drug dealers in Florida. Antonio brought so much joy into my life. I continued my education during and after I gave birth. It was hard getting up during the night having to be up for school at 5:30am, and getting a baby ready.

Grandma didn't make it easy for me. Some nights she would help, but most nights she would tell me, "You made your bed hard, and now you have to lay in it." Yes, the bed was hard, but I was determined to finish high school.

After our son Antonio, was born things changed between Boris and I. We began to fight a lot. At times it felt like we were growing apart, and at other times we were back in love. He was jealous, and so was I. I didn't want him around other females, and he would fight me if I were around other guys. Our relationship was unexplainable, but at the end of the day, we were still in love in a strange twisted way. On November 1, 1991, while Boris was laying in the bed asleep federal agents came into his Grandma home and arrested him. A lot of other people were arrested at the same time. I was so scared because I didn't know what was going to happen to Boris. I had just become a single teenage parent. I was on my way to school when the bust happened. I was afraid for Boris; he was only seventeen years old. I was afraid and ashamed, because I had just realized I was a baby momma to one of the biggest drug dealers with one of the largest operations in Florida.

I had never understood what was going on nor did I ever ask any questions. Boris did everything for Antonio; I never had to do anything. I didn't know what I was going to do. Between my Grandma and Boris doing everything for Antonio, I was clueless to everything. I didn't know what size pampers my son wore.

I called my aunt Deborah and told her what happened. She said, "You are going to be fine; you will be a good mother to your son, and you were never a part of that whole operation. You hold your head up high and become the woman I taught you to be." My auntie always had the right words to say to me and she never judged me or put me down. As time went on Antonio and I would ride with Boris's grandmother to visit him in prison. He would tell me he was coming home but after the trial was over he received three- life-sentences. I was hurt, and I didn't know how to tell Antonio his daddy was never coming home. I had just found out I was pregnant again (three months). I was afraid and I didn't know what to do. I was stressed out until the point of miscarriage, and I had never told anyone I was pregnant. I was too ashamed of what people would think or say. My mother wasn't talking to me which was no surprise. I was alone and scared, and I didn't know which way to turn. It seemed everywhere I turned I was running into a brick wall. It felt like my life was in a maze with nowhere to turn and no end.

Behind the Fist

After Boris had been in jail for awhile, I meet a man named Ahaz. He was older than me, but at the time, I was looking for protection, and financial help. My son had no strong male role model in his life, and in that lonely moment, it was easy to fall into this trap of a lie. I was young, I gotten used to fast money, and did not understand the danger I was walking into or I should say, "I did not know what the enemy had set up for me."

In the beginning things between Ahaz and I everything were good. I mean he treated me in a way I thought a woman should be treated, but then after a while he became very violent and it was scary. Ahaz began beating me for no reason at all. I remember having to sneak Antonio to the prison to visit Boris, but somehow Ahaz would find out. He would beat me, and force me to have sex with him. It had gotten to the point where I couldn't ride the school bus with my friends anymore, he would say, "The guys on the bus were trying to talk to me" How? I was riding on the bus with other teenage parents, a program that was set up for girls only. I couldn't take Antonio to my cousin Eric's house to get Antonio hair cut anymore, Ahaz said, "Your cousin Eric wants to have sex with you." Many people wondered why I would never leave him, but instead of helping me they talked about me and laughed at the situation I was in. I was scared to leave, scared to stay, and scared to die. Every time he beat me, he pulled so much of my hair out. I had to cut my hair in a style, because there were so many bare patches on the sides of my head. To this day there is still a patch of hair missing from the right side of my head. I felt like all my life, I had been in a fetal position protecting myself from the blows of other people, and not knowing how to fight back spiritually. It was hard not knowing when I going to get beaten and for what reason. There was a time he had beaten me so bad, and stepped on my head with his steel toe work boots.

One night after being at my cousin Angel house; I had enough, I had build a little courage, but I was still afraid to leave, and go home. I didn't know what Ahaz was going to do; I just never knew what mood he was going to be in. I had tried to leave him and start new relationships with others but he would come and bully them away. I met a guy Jamie. We had been seeing each other and would meet at my cousin's house. One morning Ahaz came up to Angel's house. She tried to send Ahaz to the store to get orange juice and warned us that Ahaz was outside. Unfortunately for me Ahaz was a little smarter and figured out I was in the house.

Ahaz turned his truck around and drove back to Angel's house. He knocked on her door really hard. Angel cracked the door and said, "What do you want?"

Ahaz said, "Open the door! I know Toshia is in your house!" Ahaz pushed Angel's door open I was standing behind Angel. Ahaz grabbed me by my hair, started beating me and pulled me by my hair all the way to his truck. By this time, Jamie tried to stop him, but Ahaz began making threats towards him. He pulled my hair all the way to his sister house who lived two blocks away. Once we got into her house he took me into one of the bedrooms towards the back of the house and beat me some more. He kicked me so hard in my stomach; I could taste the blood in my mouth. I stop fighting back, it was like fighting with a snake, the more I moved, the tighter he squeezed. He then forced me to have sex with him, I was thinking to myself, "Lord help me." But I was scared to make a move.

First child taken by gun point

I was four months pregnant, I was scared. Ahaz said, "You will not keep that baby" I replied, "I want my baby even if you walk away, I want my baby." Ahaz grabbed me by my hair, put his hand around my neck and said," What the fuck did I say" He threw me to the floor. I bawled in a fetal position, holding my stomach and I began to cry. He left and slammed the door. The next morning, I got up to go to school, he said, "You are not going to school today" I looked at him and I began to run down the stairs. He grabbed me by my hair, dragged me to his truck and pushed me inside. He grabbed his gun and sat it on his lap; he made me lay down in his lap with the gun next to my face while we drove. He would hit me with his fist in my head every time we would get to a red light. I could taste the salt from my tears as it rolled across my face, falling into my mouth. We pulled up to the abortion clinic in Clearwater, Florida, at that point I was shaking, I was put to sleep and the procedure was performed. I woke up and my baby was gone. I didn't know if my baby was a boy or girl, just taken out of my womb. On our way home we picked up Tonio from a friend's house. When I got home; I grabbed my son and cried.

Ahaz continued to beat me on several occasions, more than anyone will ever know. My home had become a prison. Ahaz had beaten me so bad one time; he choked me until I passed out. At times the police came, but Ahaz was the type of person who wasn't afraid of the police. He would wait until they left, come back to my house, and beat me again for calling the police. There were many times the police were called and he would have one hand around my neck and one hand around my mouth. One night after going to a high school game, some friends and I went to a club on 34th Street and 18th Avenue. I was standing in the window of the club, so I could him driving through the parking lot. I quickly left and went home, I was afraid of being beating in front of people.

When I arrived home, Ahaz pulled up around the same time. I ran into the house. Ahaz ran into the house after me, grabbed my hair, pulled me into the bedroom and said, "So you were at the club? Show me how you were dancing." I began to move from side to side. He slapped me in the mouth so hard; blood began running out from the side of my mouth. He yelled, "Dance like you were dancing in the club!" I couldn't move. I stood looking at him. Ahaz punched me so hard in my face, my head hit the wall, and I fell to the floor. He blackened my eye, it was swollen so bad until it my eye was closed. He began stepping on my head with his steel boots he wore to work, all I could do was try to scream for help, and then he would choke me until I could barely breathe.

Monday when I arrived at school my friend Tanya took me into the restroom, and began putting make up on my face, hoping it would cover the marks. Tanya looked at me with tears running down her face and say, "Toshia please leave him!"

I said to her, "I tried. He won't leave me alone, and I am afraid he will hurt anyone who might try and to help me."

On December 12, the night Grandma died, I went home and cried myself asleep. Grandma was my heart, the vessel that kept me together. When I arrived home, I didn't see Ahaz's truck, so I thought he wasn't there. When I went into my apartment, I felt his hand from behind the door. He grabbed my hair and dragged me upstairs. The beatings came so frequently, when I got upstairs, I didn't scream, I just cried and yelled my own mouth while he beat me. The day of my Grandma's funeral I begged him to allow me to go and I tried not to do anything to make him mad. That morning I got up got dressed and walked to church carrying my son on my hip. When I arrived at my church, I walked in, and began weeping. I was crying because my best friend was gone, and saying to myself, "Lord, please be with me as I go home." A part of me wanted to climb in the casket with her and lock it, but I knew my son needed me. Did I get beat on the saddest of my life? Yes, the day of my Grandma's funeral. I had so many blackouts until some days were foggy.

What do you do when you are young, and afraid, and the man is not afraid of the police and doesn't care about a restraining order? I continued to go to school because I had promised Grandma before she died that I would finish school and go to college. The beatings and sexual abuse continued until word got to my brother that Ahaz was beating on me. One day my brother, one of my cousins, and I were at my Grandparents house; when Ahaz pulled up in his truck. Ahaz called me over to his truck, I said," No!" My brother asked Ahaz to leave. Ahaz said, "I am not going anywhere until I talk to Toshia!" Ahaz and Tremyne began to argue. Ahaz told my brother he was going to kill him. Ahaz then went to his truck to get a gun (I knew he always kept a gun under the driver seat of his truck). My brother then went and got a gun. He shot Ahaz two times, my cousin and I began screaming. I had never in my life seen a person shot. Ahaz walked to his truck. He tried to start the engine but the truck wouldn't start. He got out of his truck with blood running down his arm, like a jug of water turned over, and he popped the hood to get the truck started. He then got into his truck and drove off. Later I had found out he passed out on the next block, and that's where the paramedic arrived.

Later on the police arrested my brother for attempted murder. Ahaz came to me about a month later and said," If you take me back, I will drop the chargers on your brother. I promise I would never hit you again." I didn't want my brother to spend years in prison and I was confused and didn't know what to do. I thought to myself, "My brother will be out of jail and won't be charged with attempted murder."

As time went on, Ahaz continued with his jealous ways toward me riding the bus to school, and taking Antonio to see his father. I thought to myself, "I don't know what I am doing, but I will do whatever it takes to get my brother out of jail, even if it took getting beaten and dealing with it until my brother is released from jail." My plans were to get my brother out of jail, finish school, and join the army; Ahaz would be out of my life forever.

As time went on I was excited about my high school graduation, but two weeks prior to my graduation, I had a dream of a man named David. I dreamed I was standing in the bathroom washing my face. From the side I could see someone standing with his hands in their pockets. I jumped with fear. He then looked at me and said, "Leave Ahaz alone!" I started praying because I just knew it was a nightmare. He said, "I am not here to hurt you!" I remember this man as if I had seen him today. He was brown skinned, with a medium build, tall, and he favored Ahaz a little. When I woke up I mentioned the dream to Ahaz, he looked at me crazy and said, "That was a relative of mine who died years ago." For days I was scared and shaky. I was afraid to go to sleep. I thought my apartment was haunted.

A week later I dreamed of Grandma. She was standing over me crying, I sat up in the bed and asked, "Grandma, why are you crying?" She just looked at me with her eyes overflowing with tears. As she was getting ready to speak to me, I woke up. I was puzzled because I really wanted to know what she was going to tell me.

When I got to school, I mentioned it to my teen parent teacher. She said to me," Natoshia, you are holding on to your grandma too much; let it go." I felt comfortable talking to her because, not only was she my teacher, but she was also the caseworker that handled my case when I was awarded to Grandma.

Life Changing

A month later, a day before my graduation, Ahaz called me and said, "I am on my way to your house." I could hear Antonio playing in the background. I said, "Okay," and switched back over to my friend Dee who was on the other line. We began talking about graduation and about our plans after. While on the phone with her, my front door opened, Ahaz walked up stairs with Antonio in his hand (he was wet). I dropped the phone. I screamed so loud," What the hell happened?" Ahaz said, "I was driving, and I tried to keep from hitting another car. I slammed on the brakes and Antonio's head hit the dash board!" As he was talking, I grabbed Antonio from him and I ran down stairs. I jumped in Ahaz's truck. Ahaz ran behind me, and he got in the truck. We headed toward St. Michaels' hospital. I screamed at Ahaz, "What are you doing? Take me to Bayview Hospital!" Ahaz continued going to St. Michaels'. Once we got on the ramp, I jumped out of his truck and ran into the ER screaming "My son is not breathing! I tried to perform CPR on the way, but he was not responding to me!" I was so nervous and shaking. Ahaz later came into the ER, and I asked him again, "What happened and you'd better tell me now. If my son dies I am going to kill you!" Ahaz said, "I told you. I tried to keep from hitting another car." I looked into his eyes so hard, I could see myself killing him in the hospital. Shortly after we arrived, two police officers came into the room, and asked me what had happen. I told them what Ahaz told me had happen. I could look into the officer's eyes, and I could tell they did not believe Ahaz's story; somewhere in my heart, I didn't either. I had this rage of anger in me; I lost who I was, and I didn't know the person I had become.

Many people told lies about what happened, and some put together their own story and theory. Women would write Boris, and tell him lies, and he believed them, which was to be expected. After the doctors did all they could do at St. Michaels' they transferred Antonio to Bayview hospital. I followed the ambulance, and went in the back room where he was. I held his little hands and cried so hard. I prayed to God to save my son. I said, "God, please don't let my son die. Heal him and save him!" Soon after that the doctors came in and informed me Antonio had a blood clot in his head, and they were going to do surgery on him. My body went numb. I didn't understand medical terminology or what they were saying. All I knew is my son was laying in bed, and he wasn't moving.

The doctors completed the surgery, and told me his brain was swollen, and there was a chance he was going to be in a vegetable state or he would have to learn everything all over again. I looked at the doctors with tears in my eyes. It felt like everything in me was ripped out. I couldn't breathe, I couldn't close my eyes. I just stared at the doctor with tears rolling down my face. The police continued with their investigation, and determined that Antonio was beaten in his head, chest and stomach, although Ahaz continued to deny what he had done.

The next day, the day of my high school graduation around 9 o'clock am, I received a called from a nurse at Bayview hospital, Antonio had passed away June 9. I went to the hospital, grabbed him out of the hospital bed, and I screamed, "God bring him back please God bring him back!" I felt as though someone had put hands in my chest and pulled my heart out. The pain was indescribable. A doctor couldn't cure me, I was angry with God and I had given up on praying. I didn't want to hear, "He is in a better place, God knows best, or you are going to be alright." I was not going to be all right. I was out for revenge; I had nothing to lose anymore. My mind was set on killing Ahaz, and no one was going to stop me. A voice in my head was saying, "Kill him! He murdered your baby! Chop his head off, and send it to his momma!" I began smoking weed all day every day; I had to find away to be numb. I didn't want to feel hurt anymore, and I didn't want to remember the day Ahaz brought Antonio to me not breathing, so I stayed high all the time. The day of Antonio's funeral was the worst day of my life, although a lot of people were there. The church was full, but I didn't want to go in. I just couldn't say goodbye to him. I walked slowly toward his little casket. I wanted to grab him out of the casket, but they were holding my arms. I yelled, "No! It is not fair; my baby is gone!" I held my stomach, I began to get really light headed, and a woman dressed in a nurse's uniform took me in the back because it felt like I was fainting. I wanted to stop breathing. My momma stood next to me and said, "Toshia, pull yourself together!" I asked, "What does that mean?" During the services, suicide was running through my mind, I was thinking of ways to do it and of how I was going to do it.

After the funeral everyone went back to my momma's house, I walked in the back, and I smoke weeds until I was so high. I looked at people sitting around laughing and talking about the things Antonio used to do. I was so high and numb it looked as if people's mouths were just moving, and nothing was coming out. I walked into my momma room and to lay down and cry. I didn't want to talk or laugh at anything. I wanted everyone to shut up and go home, but I couldn't tell people that; they were only doing what people do after a funerals.

While laying down, I closed my eyes. As I dosed off, it seemed as though my bed was moving, as if someone was jumping on it. I opened my eyes, looked around, and I said to myself, "Maybe I'm just high." So, I closed my eyes and it happened again. That time I knew I was high, but I wasn't that high, because I could feel my body moving as the bed was. I said to myself, "Tonio, I know that you're playing with mommy."

A few days later, Ahaz's niece came to my momma's house. She knocked on the door, and my momma answered the door. I looked out the door and told my momma, "That's Ahaz niece." My momma said, "Oh yea!" My momma opened the door very calmly and asked, "May I help you?" Ahaz's niece, "We want to know where the baby is buried." My momma said, "Hold on for a minute." She closed the door and grabbed a big stick. When she opened the door, she hit the niece so hard and said, "When I get finished with you, they are going to wonder where you are buried at!" Ahaz's niece ran, but my momma was still behind her swinging. I laughed. Later Ahaz drove by. I said to myself, "I am going to give him what he is looking for." I had set in my mind to kill him; the police were taking too long to arrest him. Family members were begging me not to get into the car. They said, "What if he kills you?" I replied, "If he kills me, bury me next to my son." It didn't matter if I lived or died. It was hard moving on with life without Antonio.

There were times I would walk every day to the cemetery to go to Antonio's grave. I would sit there and just cry. Others were continuing with their lives, but mine stopped. I would take toys to his grave, and one time I took a shovel, because in my mind, I wanted to dig him up, but I was scared to go to jail.

One night my cousin and I went to a club called Deal Lounge. I was high and I had been drinking. Someone came into the club and told me Ahaz was outside. I said to myself, "I am going to get him!" My cousin and I walked outside and walked up on him. We started beating him. We beat him until he jumped in his truck, the side of his rail from his truck was hanging on the ground as he drove off. Soon after, St. Petersburg Police had enough evidence on Ahaz to make an arrest. I was happy, but it wasn't enough. In the meantime, I had gotten a summer job with my cousin working at a Community Center. As I was walking to work one day, I meet Dell. It was strange because his truck looked like Ahaz's; it was the same colors but opposite. People were lying and saying I was riding around in the truck with Ahaz, but he was in jail. Although Ahaz and Dell had the same complexion, they did not look alike. But that's society for you; having a story for everything whether it's the truth or a lie.

The Trial

A year later, Dell and I continued to see each other, and I had just found out I was pregnant. The next day I went to for the sentencing for Ahaz. My momma told me not to go, but I wanted to be there every at step to make sure Ahaz never got out of jail. The attorney asked me, "Do you want Ahaz to get the death penalty or life in prison without parole?" I'm thinking death. My momma said, "The Lord will deal with him; you don't want his death to be on your hands when judgment come." I looked at her; I wanted to say so badly, "I'm sure the Lord will understand. I will deal with that on judgment day when it comes." But of course, I did what my momma told me, and I told the attorney, "Life without parole!" Dell and I walked into the courtroom.

Ahaz's mother and sister were sitting inside. I sat behind them. The judge sentenced Ahaz to life without parole. I screamed, "Yes!" His mother looked back with a frown on her face. I didn't care; at least her son was still alive. He got life without parole, and I got life without my son. After everything was over, Dell and I stood up and proceeded to walk out. Ahaz's family was walking behind us. All of a sudden Ahaz's mother reached over and pulls my hair. I turned around and started fighting. I forgot where I was, Dell grabbed Ahaz's mother because he was trying to protect his unborn child I was carrying. I was thinking to myself, "You're hitting me. You're trying to kill my unborn child!" I am pregnant and her son murdered my child! I am going to beat the black dust off of her!" I was ready for whatever. Ahaz wasn't hand-cuffed, and he was headed towards me yelling, "Stop hitting my momma!" Dell hit him so hard he fell across the table. The bailiffs grabbed Ahaz and his mother.

Ahaz's sister came running over to me. I picked up a chair and threw it at her. At that point, I remembered I was pregnant. I began to have pain at the bottom of my stomach, and I thought to myself, "They are trying to steal the life of another child from me!" One of the bailiffs said, "How can they come at you, when it's clearly shown her son murdered your child. I don't understand that. Why is she mad at you? He did it, not you. You have a right to protect your unborn child, and she looked at Dell and said, "You as a citizen have the right to break up a fight." The bailiff called EMS, and they took me to Bayview Hospital. Ahaz's mother was told she was under arrest for hitting a pregnant woman. She stated, "She was having a heart attack" and was taken to Eastpointe Hospital.

My momma was home watching The Young n the Restless; when a newsbreak flashed on TV. She said, "All she saw was Dell and me swinging and fighting!" Her phone began ringing off the hook. People calling to tell her what happened in the courtroom. After I was rushed to the hospital, nurses monitored my baby, she was Ok. My momma came to the hospital she and said, "They better be glad I wasn't there; I would have killed her!" She turned, looked at me, and said, "Where is she?" I said, "When they told her I was pregnant, and she was under arrest for hitting a pregnant woman. She pretended to have a heart attack and they took her to another hospital." I thought to myself, "How can a family be so devilish. It is bad enough I had to bury my baby as a result of what your child did, and now you want to add to the pain I am already going through." Yes, Ahaz was sentenced to life without parole, but I was sentenced to life without Antonio.

During my Pregnancy with O'neisha

As time went on my pregnancy became hard for me; I continued to cry and think about Antonio. From time to time, I would dream about him. I would dream we were playing together in a field of beautiful yellow flowers. During my pregnancy I wanted to know what I was having, but the doctors couldn't see what the sex was. So, one night I dreamed I was sitting at a table with my head down, when I looked up and saw my grandma. She stood staring at me, and then she walked around the corner. I followed her. She pulled up a chair and sat down in front of me. She looked at me and smiled. I heard a small voice giggling behind me. I turned and looked. It was Antonio, and he was running around with a little girl. They were holding hands, playing with each other. Antonio ran to me and jumped in my arms. I looked at him with tears in my eyes, and said, "Antonio, I am so sorry. I miss you so much."

Antonio said, "Mommy, I know; I know." He kissed me; he jumped down, and continued to play with the little girl. I finally got a look at the little girl. It was like my face was on hers. She was dark skinned with long hair, and she had on a white dress, white ruffle socks, and white church shoes. She was so pretty.

Then I saw white smoke, Grandma stood up, she grabbed both of their hands, and walked away. I yelled, "Don't go! Please don't go!" They didn't look back; they continued walking until they vanished. I woke up with tears in my eyes but with joy. Antonio is with Grandma, and I knew right then I was having a little girl. I went to Wal-Mart and put little girl things on lay-away. My momma and Dell said, "You don't know what you having." I said, "Yes I do. Grandma and Antonio showed her to me last night." They looked at me as if I was crazy. I said, "I am going to name her O'neisha."

On March 10, 1995, I gave birth to O'neisha. She weighed 6 pounds 12 ½ ounces. My cousin Peaches and my momma were in the delivery room. I was so excited and full of joy because I was blessed to be a mother again. After O'neisha was born, I took her to the graveyard. I said, "Antonio, you have a little sister now. Her name is O'neisha Kyana." She just looked around with those, big pretty eyes. We sat there for about an hour. I told tell her all about her brother. I got up, put Nique in her car seat, and drove off, and as I was driving tears rolled down my face. I didn't look back, because it was too painful; I felt that if I looked back. I would be looking back at pain. I knew it was time for me to get my life together, and be a good mother to Nique (the nickname my brother gave her) Tremyne said, "She looks like a Nique." I never knew what that meant, but we began calling her that. I thought it was cute.

The Unexpected

A few years later on September 27, 1997, Dell and I got married. With the family friend making visits to cheat with my husband and on her husband, my marriage began turning down a dark road. I later gave birth to a little boy name An'treyon "Trey" Sermon, he was born on January 30, 1999, with all the drinking and cheating, I filed for divorced in June 2001. I tried to make our marriage work, but with the family friend (his mistress) coming to visit from Jacksonville, Florida almost every weekend, the devil had stolen my marriage, which ended in a divorce.

A'miya

After two years went by, I ran into an old boyfriend. He and I would talk for hours on the phone; I was kind of scared of getting involved with anyone else. But I felt well, since I knew him, I guessed it would be okay to give it a chance.

I called my cousin Peaches and said, "Ya Boy is back in town." She said, "Girl, I know. He has been looking for you!"

I told her, "He is a Sergeant in the Army now, but girl. I don't know if I really want to see anybody else." Peaches giggled and hung up the phone. Later on that night, he and I went out on a date. I had dropped my kids off to my best friend Tanya's house. One thing led to another, and a month later I was pregnant. I had just started a job at the hospital. I didn't know what I was going to do with three children. I told him I was pregnant, and he thought I was playing until he came home and saw I was showing. He rubbed my stomach and stared at me. I asked, "What are you looking at?" He said, "You are really pregnant with my child."

I said, "Yeah, it looks that way." As time went on my pregnancy began to get scary to me. Different things I was experiencing I had never experienced before with my other children. Well, I went into labor very early, twenty-seven weeks into my pregnancy, my water broke. None of the doctors at the hospital would let me delivery her. All they kept telling me was that they were waiting on her lungs to mature. Now, in the meantime, my baby was inside of me with no fluid, was getting sick, and she was getting sick. My hair was falling out, I was blowing up, I was breaking out in hives, and it felt as though I was near my own death.

I could remember at times it felt as if my bed was lifting high in the sky, and I was surrounded around white clouds. When the nurse walked in to check on me, it felt like the bed immediately came down really fast. I was so scared. I just stared at the nurse as she walked in to take my vital signs. I looked at her and asked, "Do you know when they are going to do my C-section?"

She replied, "I don't know; it's the doctor's decision."

Later on my momma came to see me. I looked at her and said, "Momma, please make them take this baby out of me. I feel like I am dying." My momma walked to the nurse's station, and I could hear her talking really loud. She had a way of getting her point across to anybody. She asked, "What is going on that these damn doctors? Why aren't they taking this baby out? There is no fluid, and my daughter is getting worst. Have you ever seen the movie John Q? Well, there's going to be another John Q up in here, if somebody doesn't make a decision, and I could care less whom in charge. Now, you can call the police or any damn body you want too."

A few minutes later, a doctor came in to check me. I can remember her saying, "Oh, my God; everything inside her is green." They rushed me into the operating room, where they performed a C- section. When I had her, I looked at her, and she was so beautiful. She was tiny, and had head full of hair, and she had those Chinese looking eyes. She looked like her dad. I called A'miya's dad and told him, I had the baby. Not once did he come see her. A'miya was rushed to the Children's Hospital next door to the hospital where I had given birth. Of course, A'miya was born sick, from them leaving her in me for 10 days.

One morning around 4:00 am, I received a call from a nurse, who told me to come to the hospital fast, A'miya was dying. The hospital staff had done everything they could for her, when she arrived to them, she was already sick. I jumped in my car, and ran every red light I could to get to the hospital. When I arrived, I walked into ICU for infants. She was on a breathing machine. I rubbed her legs and held her little fingers. The nurse looked at me and asked, "Are you ready?"

I said, "Give me a second; I just want to kiss her and hold her for ten minutes."

She looked at me and said, "Take your time Ms. Mitchell"; I called my best friend, and said, "A'miya is gone!" She began to cry and said, "I am on my way!"

I called her dad and told him, "Your daughter has passed away" He said, "Okay."

I said, "Okay? You Bastard! That's all you can say, Okay!" My best friend grabbed the phone and began to curse him out. He just hung up the phone as if he didn't care. My best friend washed and dressed A'miya and brought her to me, I held her for hours, and I couldn't let her go. I begged God like I had begged God for Antonio's life on the way to the hospital; please don't let my baby die.

A'miya's dad never showed up to her funeral or never did. He never acknowledged she was born. A week after the funeral, I returned to work; I just wanted to be strong for my surviving children. I thought to myself, "Here is a man who proclaims to fight for his country but will not fight for his own daughter's life. How can he save a stranger's life and turn his back on his daughter? Isn't that something for a solider going to war?" I prayed to God to release in my heart forgiveness towards him. I forgave him; he apologized over and over for what he did. I told him I forgave him a long time ago, and it's God he has to deal with, because my baby knew I loved her, and she knew I was there every day. Even a few years later he sent an email stating apologizing.

I said," I forgave you. It's ok."

He said," I am not that type of person" I replied, "I understand."

Good bye Momma

As time went on, my momma and I began to get closer, she would have cookouts at her house. I loved spending time and staying the night with my little sisters; my kids enjoyed it more. My momma had a pool in her backyard, and the kids would swim while my momma would put some meat on the grill and drink her Michelob short. Soon after that, my momma moved into a duplex apartment she didn't like it, but at the time she had to get what she could afford.

One day my momma called me and said," I want to go to the grocery store. They have snow crabs on sale." I said, OK, I will be there in a few minutes"

We sat and talked. My momma was telling me she was so very proud of me, and she apologized for everything that we had been through. We talked about some really deep stuff. It was weird, because she was telling me what to do and how to do things regarding life and being a mother.

The next day I went to church. My best friend and I made a decision we were going to get saved. I had told my momma I would come by after church.

She told me she had cooked collard greens, mac and cheese, rice, ox tails, and corn bread. During service, my two sisters came running into church screaming, "Ma is dead!"

I said, "What!" I ran out of church, when I arrived, the paramedic was performing CPR on her. I knew by looking at her she was gone. I screamed, "NO! I just talked to her." I squeezed my fist as tight as I could, looked up in the sky, grabbed my two sisters, and followed the paramedic to the hospital, where she was pronounce dead. I called family members, and they all came down to the hospital. Everyone was crying. I knew I had to pull myself together because I had my two younger sisters I needed to be strong for. They were only sixteen and fourteen years old. My brother had been shot six times three months prior, and I had just lost my daughter A'miya six months before, so everything was on me to handle.

When I arrived at the hospital, my momma was laying on the table. I held her hands and looked up. I just couldn't believe it. I grabbed my youngest sister Ashley, as she laid her head on my shoulders, crying, and my other sister Shakita, stood over momma crying. After we left the hospital my sisters and I went back to momma house and ate her last meal as a family.

The next day I called the funeral home to make preparations for my mom's funeral. She had no life insurance, and I was at a dead end. My sisters and I went to our mom's house to see if we could find money she may have had hidden.

My mom was good at hiding money around the house. We found nothing, so I looked in her car, and in the trunk of her car was $2500. I looked up at the sky and said, "Thank you Jesus." It was a start. I called the funeral home the cemetery needed $1500 before they could do anything else. I bought clothes for my mom and sisters and took the rest to the funeral home.

The next day I called my cousin Peaches, and told her I need her help, she said, "Sis, what do you need me to do?"

I said, "I don't know where to begin."

Peaches said, "I'm down for whatever."

I said, "Okay. I need you to go with me to the funeral home. I want to dress my momma, because she was not an old lady, and I don't want her looking like an old lady."

Peaches said, "Okay, I will go in and measure her head to make a nice wig." After Peaches measured my momma's head, I went to Central Plaza and bought a white and silver dress suit, silver accessories, and a silver purse. I picked out a white and silver casket with white roses on top. I wanted my momma to look as beautiful as I could; it's wasn't hard to do, because she was a beautiful woman anyway.

I called the funeral home and advised them I would be dressing my mom and bringing her clothes. The next day Peaches and I went to the funeral home, and walked into the back room where my momma was lying on a table. I grabbed

Peaches' hand, and she looked at me and said, "Sis we can do this." I looked at her and said, "I know; it's hard." We walked slowly towards momma. Peaches did her hair; we put on her clothes and did her makeup. I polished her nails, while Peaches was putting on her stockings.

The shock didn't hit me until the funeral employees came in, picked her up, and placed her in the casket. I fell to my knees screaming, because I knew at that moment, it was "Good-bye, Momma."

When my momma's funeral was over, my dad, Darrell came to my brother and me and said, "Pop's isn't going anywhere; I am going to stay here and get my life together, because Tremyne needs me right now. Toshia, you have always been the strong one." I said, "I am tired of being strong. I need somebody to be strong for me right now." Darrell said, "Baby girl, I am here now, and your daddy loves the both of you." Tremyne looked at Darrell said, "Okay." I looked at Darrell, and for some reason, I found trust and gave him that chance to be a father again.

After the funeral, it was time to get our mom's furniture out of her apartment. People who offered to help were nowhere to be found, and some did not answer their phones. I looked at my sisters and said, "We are not going to worry about it; we will do it ourselves." I rented a moving truck, I asked my niece mother to drive the truck because I was really scared to drive that big truck. My sisters, my kid's and I lifted everything from the living room set to the washers and dryers. We loaded everything on the truck; my niece mother drove the truck to my new house. We unloaded everything by ourselves. My niece mother drove the truck back to my apartment. We lifted everything, loaded the truck again, and took all my furniture to my new house. It was a lot of hard work, but God made a way.

Two weeks later, after I had just gotten home from work. I was cooking dinner for my sisters and my two children, when the phone rang it was my aunt on the other line. She asked, "Toshia, are you sitting down?" I said, "Yes." But I really wasn't, because I was preparing myself for what she was about to tell me." She said, "Your father was just killed in a car accident."

I said, "Okay" and I hung up the phone. A minute later my father's sister called and said, "Toshia, your daddy is dead; he was on his way out of town, and he was killed in Leesburg County. The state trooper called and said, "He died instantly, and every bone in his body was broken."

I said, "Okay."

My aunt asked, "Are you okay? Toshia, you know its okay to cry." I said, "I'm fine." I hung up the phone, laid on the bed and stared at the wall; as tears rolled down my face. I thought to myself, "What in the world have I done so bad to deserve all of this?" I felt numb, and I couldn't move. My sisters came running in the room, and

Shakita asked, "Toshia, what's wrong?"

I said, "My daddy is dead." I screamed as loud as I could. I said, "What is wrong with my life; why is all this happening to me? Is God that mad at me? What could I have done to God to deserve all of this? Does someone have witchcraft on me?" I had so many questions in my head, and I didn't know where to turn or who to turn to. I was still was trying to be strong for my sisters, my brother, and my own kids.

During my daddy's funeral, Grandma Georgia walked over to us and said, "Dry your tears and stop crying; it's going to be all right." I thought to myself, "What's that? Nothing is all right anymore." As I sat there staring at my daddy's body, everything crossed my mind. Here I am twenty-seven years old, I had buried two children, I had lost the only woman that truly cared about me, I lost my brother Vernon, my momma, now two weeks later I am staring at my father's body in a casket. I couldn't cry anymore; I felt my body was all out of tears.

After the funeral home limo was missing. I looked at my sister Tenisha and said, "Where is your grandma?"

She said, "She was in the last limo behind us." When we arrived at my uncle Marvin house, Grandma Georgia was still nowhere to be found. About ten minutes later the limo arrives, grandma Georgia got out of the limo with a brown bag in her hand. She paid the limo driver $20 to stop by the liquor store. My sister looked at me and said,

"That is your Grandma." And I just looked, dropped my head down, and walked over to Grandma Georgia and gave her a kiss.

After

I moved to Tampa, Florida, to begin a new life with my children. I moved with a friend. I was unemployed. I was receiving $13.29 in child support and nine months later after going back to court and my kids father's still playing games with his employment I began to receive was less than $200 a month for child support for two children. I was driving in a truck the repo company was looking for, but I held my head up high, and I kept going. I applied for housing, and I was able to get a three-bedroom, two-bathroom house. It wasn't the best, but it wasn't the worst. It was a blessing for me and my kids. I began working for a well-known insurance company, and after three months I was hired permanent, signed up to go to college and six months later I was promoted to an EDI Analyst. I started classes in fall 2005. I still made mistakes in relationships and dating ungodly men. I begin drinking and taking pills to go the sleep. In my mind, I thought it was helping me. I went to work every day dressed nice but wounded on the inside. I was running from my past, I was hiding within myself, and I did not want memories in St. Petersburg, Florida. I hated the sight of being there; it was full of hurt and pain.

Five years later I moved back to St. Petersburg thinking that everything had changed. I listened to my kid's father saying he was going to be there more for Trey and Nique, of course that was lie. I thought that family love was going to be better, and I started missing family. St. Pete was still the same; nothing had changed, I began to feel uncomfortable in my spirit, and my soul felt tormented. I found myself going to the graveyards every other day, and I was beginning to feel depressed.

My best friend moved to Tallahassee, Florida, and my life wasn't the same. I stopped dating for a while, and focused on getting my life in order. I started going to church more and getting into the word. I found a church called Lion of Judah. I had never met an understanding pastor in all my life. He was very easy to talk to, and wasn't afraid to tell me about the word of God. His wife is a woman with a lot of wisdom and very easy to talk to as well.

Soon after I met a guy who lived in Tallahassee, we talked on the phone everyday for about five months before we actually met each other in person. I began to drive to Tallahassee to visit my best friend almost every other weekend. My kids enjoyed the drive, we were getting away from St. Pete, and it felt good.

Tremyne Last Six Months

Tremyne had turned himself in and the judge sentenced him to four years in prison. Tremyne was in a prison close to Tallahassee, Florida. While going to Tallahassee, his daughter's mother and I would visit every Saturday. Tremyne became very sick because of the lack of care in prison, bed sores were all over his lower body, and they stopped giving him physical therapy (which cause his legs to become paraplegic and we were unable to move Tremyne without him being in a lot of pain). He went from walking into the prison to dying from lack of care.

Seeing my brother in the situation was very hurtful and tormenting; I never thought nurses and doctors could mistreat people regardless of being in prison. In January while going to visit my brother, a nurse told us they were only giving Tremyne six months to live. Tears rolled down my eyes, and I looked down at him. Tremyne did not want to accept what the doctor had said. Tremyne looked at me and said, "Don't tell nobody what the doctor said. You know how our family is; they will go around telling lies."

I looked at him and said, "Okay." We cried and prayed together. He looked at me and said, "Sis I love you, but I am tired. I am going through it, and I don't know how much longer I can hold on. I am trying to be strong and stay alive for you." On April 1, I had a dream about my brother. I saw him in a white casket and a white suit. I woke up and told my sister. "Tremyne is not going to live much longer, and we don't have much time!" At that moment, I decided I had to be closer to my brother. I let my job go; I packed up my things, and moved to Tallahassee, Florida. I visited my brother every weekend and when he was transferred to the hospital in Jacksonville, Florida. I visited every weekend. Tremyne and I laughed, talked and prayed. We had a deep conversation. He still cracked jokes and still tried to remain himself, even though he knew he was dying of bone cancer.

When I went to see him at the hospital in Jacksonville, Tremyne said, "Sis, I saw Grandma, Momma, and Antonio. I'm tired, I have given my life to God, and he has forgiven me for all my sins." With tears in my eyes, I said Tremyne, its okay to go home. You don't have to be strong for me anymore. I am going to be all right. I know you are tired; go and be with the Lord."

Tremyne looked at me and said," If anything comes out of this; make sure you, Shakita, Ashley and my kids are taken care of, because some people say they will be with you through thick and thin. You will never see them again. I am not going to worry about it; I love you and thank you for giving up everything to be with me."

I looked at him, and even though there were a lot of lies being said while going back and forth to visit my brother, I don't regret it and I would do it again. You are my brother, and I don't care what anybody says." I kissed him on the forehead and walked out of the room. As I walked to the elevator, I turned to look back, and I could see he was still watching me. He watched me all the way to elevator to see if I was going to cry. I blew him a kiss and walked on the elevator. As the doors closed, I broke down and cried as hard as I could. I asked myself, "Lord what do I do now?" When I got in the car, I put in one of my favorite songs, "I Gonna Be Ready", I put the song on repeat, and cried and cried until I had to pull over, and began throwing up. I screamed, "Lord help me; I don't know what to do! I can't let go! I can't let go!" I beat the steering wheel of the car, held my head back for a minute to catch my breath, it felt like I was losing everything.

I began driving, my mind was too foggy for a while I didn't know where I was, I just drove until I saw things that looked familiar to me. I was in Tallahassee at a grocery store. I got scared because that had happened to me before after A'miya passed away. I didn't know where I was, I drove until I saw something that looked familiar, and I ended up downtown St. Pete. God still kept me.

It was hard because family members lied and had a board meeting about me. "They said I was moving to be with a man." No one took the time to find out why I was moving or even asked how Tremyne was doing. The ones who were talking never took the time to write him a letter or even visit to give family support. They didn't see the condition he was in or they weren't there when he coded and was revived.

They weren't holding his hands as he was taking his last breath. They didn't go to Tallahassee to fight the board of commission for his rights to come home. But they had so much to say. I still held my head up high, kept my brother secret, and stood by his side until the end.

On July 2, 2009 at 10:00 pm I got a call from his daughter's mother. She said, "He is gone!" I hung up the phone, screamed, I cried. It felt like a knife had gone through my heart and come out of my back. I lay on the floor, and my kids came running in the room, screamed "He is gone! He is gone! Oh, Lord he's gone!" I called my aunts, sisters, and other family members. Peaches called me and said, "Sis, you know I am here again."

I said, 'I know. You are one person I can always count on." Peaches said, "What do you need me to do?" I said, "I want you and my sister to make sure Tremyne is dressed nice. I want him in a white suit I saw, a white casket, a white derby hat, and his cane. I have to go back to Tallahassee to take care of some business, so make sure Eric cut his hair and give him a shave. His daughter's mother will do the programs, and make sure the shirts are ready for everyone to pick up." We all came together to make sure he was dressed and put away nice. My brother had no insurance, and everything again was left for me to pay. I knew God was going to work it out. I love my brother, and he was everything to me. Although we had our ups and downs as all brothers and sisters do, at the end, we always came together as one to make a fist to fight all battles together. I know my brother is with our parents and especially our grandparents. For some reason before he passed, he began looking like granddaddy. That night when I went to sleep, I had a dream about a beautiful little girl. She came up to me, and began singing and turning around in circles very slowing. She was singing "The Storm Is Over." I looked with tears in my eyes, and her mother came up and said, "I am sorry; she is always singing to people."

 I said," It's okay; let her sing." I woke up with tears is my eyes, and I began to praise God. I looked up the words to the song, and the words were comfort for me.

After my brother's funeral, I went back to Tallahassee, I felt as though my job was done in Tallahassee. The passion was gone, but I knew I did not want to go back to St. Pete; that was out of the question. I talked to a cousin who was living in Georgia, and I told her I wanted to move. She said, "Cuz my doors are always open. If you come I can show you where to find a place to live and a job." I said, "Okay." The next week I packed up our things and moved to Georgia with my kids. Again, some family members still talked about me. They accused me of things I didn't do, lied about me, and talked about me." They said, "I had moved to be with a man in Georgia. It wasn't the will of God, and that I wasn't going to be blessed." I thought to myself, "God said in his word, "He will never leave you nor forsake you, so you to tell me God is only in St. Pete?" I began to think to myself, the same city I have been in hell all my life, where I am unhappy, and my soul and spirit feels tormented? You mean to tell me God wants me there?" The devil is a lie. I realized some people didn't care if I was unhappy in my situations; they just wanted to have something to talk about.

I remembered what a Pastor said to me in Tallahassee, "Leaving Florida will be the best decision you have ever made. Some people will be mad and talk about you, but the ones who are talking to do not want to see you prosper. When you cross the Florida, everything will fall off. Continue with your book, because a lot of women have to hear what you have to say. People will be healed." My best friend and I looked at each other and began praising God.

I prayed and asked God to guide me and be with my children and me. One Sunday morning I was looking at television, a well-known Pastor was preaching about the will of God. When he said, "Let no one tell you you're out of the will of God. There is no such thing as not being in the will of God. Job was in the will of God." That was all the confirmation I needed to hear. I began to praise God because, at that moment, everything people were saying became unimportant to me. I am in a new place where I don't have to worry about what family members have to say or what they are going to lie about next. It's didn't matter to me, and I didn't care anymore, because I am living my life for God and being a mother to my children. It's behind me now, and we are happy with the decision to move to Georgia.

After we moved to Georgia in July 2009, a little fear sat in, I really didn't know what I was going to do, and everything was new. In August 2009, we moved into our apartment. My furniture was still in a storage unit in Florida, and I had no money to get it out at the time. So I went to Wal-Mart and bought blow-up beds. My children and I slept on them for six months, until I was able to get my furniture and bring it to Florida in February 2010. Living in Georgia has been an awesome experience. I've learned to trust and depend on God more than ever. Trey is playing football, and Neisha is cheerleading. I still get scared sometimes because I have no family here beside me and sometimes I feel like I want to move to Tampa. Moving to Georgia was the best experience I could have ever given my children. Many people can prophesy to you and tell you what the Lord said (in their words), and I am not saying everyone is incorrect. But is "It for their good or benefit" or is it a true word from God? God would not take you where the Holy Spirit wouldn't keep you. God is good, and at this point in life, I realize God will remove you out of your comfort zone to put you in a place to put all your trust in him only.

My story is not to put anyone down; it was a part of my life! It is about true forgiveness, restoration, deliverance. Having faith even though you may be going through your storm or have been through the storm, just know that God is still on the throne (Hebrews 12:2, NIV). He sits high and looks low. Trust God, and allow him to be the head of your life. My life is a testimony to those who have been through or are going through. Just know if God can heal me, he will and can heal you. Trust God!

God is God, all day and everyday

Prayer changes things!

"I Know"

I know what I know when I know who I am. Who I knew was battered, abused,

confused and misused.

Searching deep inside my soul with nowhere to run and nowhere to hide

What I did not know was God's creation of a virtuous woman.

Standing still in the midst of it all, in his presence; kneeling down with my hands

stretched high, while the tears rolled down my face.

Saying, "Help me God." and he did.

I know what I know when I found my creator that knows who I am.

"Interference"

He interfered into a plan that God designed just for me; I allowed it.

Not understanding a dangerous zone, I entered, only focusing on the men I desired, but

not the plans of God. Tall, thick, dark, and handsome he sent me.

It was interference. Forgetting my entire morals Grandma had taught me.

Only to be cheated with and cheated on. It was interference.

Running to the clubs, looking for what I thought was Mr. Right now.

It was interference. "Who was I running to?" I asked myself.

It was interference.

"Like a Parasite"

Like a parasite coming to kill, steal and destroy; it moves around slowly in your body and grows rapidly with the increase of sin in your life; it has eyes and ears. This parasite goes everywhere you go, eats whatever you eat, and lives in the pit of your soul, down in your belly.

Bloated from the sin that has been deposited in your body from sin, constipated from not being delivered, feeling fatigued because of Satan eating away nutrition's God has deposit. It continues to grow with every sin you commit.

Calling all his friends to manifest into your body (Galatians 5:17-21, NIV) like adultery, murder, lying, lust, fornication, hatred, strife, sedition, heresy, variance, emulations, lasciviousness, idolatry, witchcraft, and darkness.

No fiber supplement or colon cleansing can kill this parasite. You cannot call your provider for medication.

Your provider may not understand this move of the enemy.

This parasite has grown and it's out to kill you. It doesn't want to leave you, it wants our soul, it doesn't want to be alone; it wants your life to be dirty, with unclean spirits, and it wants you to live in darkness. Only one provider can save you from this parasite, and his name is Jesus. He will send your body, spirit, and soul through a detoxification and destroy the parasite that Satan has developed in your body.

He will heal you. The only medication you need is to fall down on your knees, confess

your sin, seek his face, and ask for forgiveness

(Isaiah 1; 18, NIV) Your only co pay is your faith. He will heal you; you don't have to

worry about being Baker Acted into psychiatric hospital or being on medication. God

said," His word will bring healing, Psalm 107:2, NIV" Nothing can defeat the blood of

Jesus; not even Satan. So will you see Dr. Jesus or will you allow the parasites to

continue to grown, develop inside your body, and eat away at your soul?

"If"

If you know what I know, what are you going to do?

If you know that paying tithe will increase your blessing, now what are you going to

do? If you know that prayer changes things, now what are you going to do?

If you know that God is the peace that passes all understanding, now what are you

going to do? If you know that in the midst of your circumstances that

God will save and deliver you as he did

Daniel in 6:1-28, NIV and for the woman with the issue of blood for twelve years in

Luke 8:43-48, NIV, now what are you going to do?

If you know that God is your only judge and you are forgiven for all your sins seventy

times seven Matthew 18:21-22, NIV, now what are you going to do?

If you know the bible says in James 5:16, NIV, that confessing your sins to each other

and praying for each other so that you may be healed, and that the prayer of the

righteous man is powerful and effective, now what are you going to do?

If you know that God will make your enemies your footstool; so what are you worried

about, and what are you going to do?

If you know that no weapon form against you shall prosper Isaiah 54:17, NIV ,and God shall

apply all your needs according to his riches and his glory Philippians 4:9, NIV, now

what are you going to do?

If you know that God is coming back and he is looking for his bride without a spot or

wrinkle, now what are you going to do?

If you know you are not saved and won't be delivered when God comes back, and that

you will be roommate with Satan for eternity, what are you going to do?

Now you know what I know, what are you going to do?

The choice is yours...

"The Key"

As I walked down a long hallway, I saw a key. It was shining so bright I could barely

see. There were many doors on my right and many on my left. I thought to myself,

"Which door would this key fit or what is this key for"

So, I walked down the hall, confused about what I could see. I stepped out on faith

and tried to open every door I could see. Every door I open was dark and empty, so I

prayed and had faith for what the Bible mentions. As I walked slowly to the last door, I

squeezed the knob tightly, I opened it slowly, only to see the room was very bright. So

bright, I could barely see what was ahead of me. So, I walked in slowly only to be at

the feet of Jesus, the right hand of our Father. I was so glad to see I'm at the hem of his

garments. I was set free, loosed from the bondage and unforgiveness I held so deeply.

Prayer is the key, and faith unlocks all doors. As Jesus reminds me, I had the key all

along to open every door locked in front of me.

"Out with the Old"

Out with the old and in with the new was an old saying I always knew.

Married to a man my mother warned me about, only to be hard headed with a doubt.

Ten years in a relationship, miserable and unhappy, he drank, cheated and stayed out

partying all night. There was a child born that I found out. I was an unknown

stepmother to two children he had buried inside. He kept them hidden as he smiled

and lied to keep us together, not knowing his past would come to the light. They were

buried alive as he hid them with shame, made me think they were his cousins as the

family member took the blame. It all came to the light, as I prayed it would. I learned

to lean on Jesus as he showed me the way. His family hates, me and I don't care; they

don't breathe my fresh air. I am happy as I've moved on; the best decision, my mother

knew all along. I am a proud single mother, and I am not ashamed;

I know Jesus will show me the way. Out with the old, and in with the new, the best

decision my mother knew.

"From Younger to Older"

I don't know if you don't teach me.

Teach me to fish so I can feed my generation spiritually to come.

I can only inherit what I am taught. If you don't teach me, how will I know if I'm

growing into a so-called hoochie mama? I head down the wrong path, but you talk

about me, you point fingers at me, and you tell me I am nothing. You never taught me

to read the Bible, yet you claim to know God. You never taught me how to become a

young woman, yet you are a woman. I had a baby at a young age, yet you had child

before marriage and still wore a white dress. You said I would become a dropout. I

graduated and even have a Masters degree.

What is wrong with this picture? Did you forget your past?

Are your skeletons so deep God cannot reveal them?

Who taught you? Or were you born a saint?

Why can't you teach me how to be a mother; a woman? Help me to understand what

lesson, you are holding back from me. God helped me accept the things I am unable to

change and the wisdom to make a difference. God gave me favor, grace, mercy, and he

changed my life and forgave me for all my sins (as he did you). He took the negative

and turned it into positive. He turned bad into good and showed me right from wrong.

I praised him. I worship him. Through it all, he had mercy on my soul and designed a virtuous woman within me. I'm not what you thought and I did not down the road you

spoke in my life.

"Forgetful Church Folks"

Now that I am saved and a Christian, God has blessed me with my Bachelor degree,

working towards my Masters, and I am now I am the owner of a successful company.

My salary is six figures, I am married, and I have a big home. God has truly blessed me

and forgiven me for all my sins. He has turned my dark into light and moved

mountains out of my way.

Now that I am saved, I don't have time to talk to you. As a matter of fact, I am going to

talk about you. I don't have time to teach you how to be a Christian, what the word of

God says, or how to be a mother. You are beneath me now. I walk past my employees at

work with my nose held high, and I don't even say good morning, but only to certain

ones who kiss my butt and tell me everything. I show favoritism at work; I have it

going on. I no longer have to depend on the welfare system anymore. My bank account

is large and don't ask me for any money, because I think you are lazy. I don't have time

to teach you about tithing or about how to find God for yourself. Oh! Did I tell you I

don't have time to teach you about the Bible and about what the word of God says? I

don't remember my past, and I forgot about the skeletons that are still in my closet. I

think you are the devil; but I still don't have time to help show you the way, because I

think you are trapped in darkness. Your spirit doesn't agree with mine. You don't go to

church; you go to the clubs. You're sleeping around with different people: "*I was a virgin when I got married."* You've committed adultery, you're just a sinner, and you

are going to hell. I just don't want to have anything to do

with you. I don't have time to tell you the truth.

Just a few years ago, I was where you are today. I was in your shoes; I walked your

path, and the same God who saved me can save you. I won't tell you that because I

want to judge you, the way you're wearing your pants hanging down or the way

you're wearing your shorts short and your short skirts.

I used to sell drugs, I cheated on my wife, I robbed people, I have a baby my wife

knows nothing about. I have slept with the deacon in the church or maybe the pastor.

When your wife is out, and I see her I am going to tell her everything about you on the

down low, and then I am going to try to holler at her.

I have been in prison, and I am also on the down low. I have smoked drugs.

I have cheated on my husband and even had a child that he thinks is his. I had children

before I was married. I've murdered people spiritually, I sold my body to make ends

meet, and I have had so many men in my life I have lost count

(A lot you will never know about).

I don't want to tell you my testimony, because I forgot where I came from.

"Switched DNA"

Here I am in somewhat of a Sarah and Hagar situation, my husband has a child from another woman. I am unable to bare him any children. We've adopted a son that will reap the harvest of our success, not hers. She has had the baby; it's a boy. I am jealous and upset. Yeah! She is a beautiful, but I am better, because I am successful with my doctor's degree, and I have more to offer my husband. The baby is born, and it is time to have a DNA test. I need to meet with her husband, so we meet at a local restaurant by the Gandy Bridge. He is upset, and he wants the child to be his, and so do I. So we decided to come up with a plan. I am successful, and I know people in higher place. She's not as smart as me, and she will never know. So her husband and I arrange to have a DNA test done.

We make arrange for the DNA to be switched so the child will come out to be her husband's and I can move on living life with my husband.

Nine years have gone by, and the child is still on my mind, so I'm peep inside because everyone says the child looks like my husband. They have the same character. He is very smart, he's very good at football and for some strange reason he wants to attend the same university my husband graduated from "without knowing that." I have a picture of this child; I' m talking to people asking around. She finds out and confronts my husband; he is unaware of our plan. I called her now her ex-husband; we both contact her not knowing we called minutes apart. I have to see how much she knows or

if she really knows

anything. I have my husband on my end wrapped around my finger, so he will believe

me. I need to make sure her ex-husband can convince her of the same. But I never

realized when her brother was shot seven times her ex-husband confessed everything

to him, thinking he was going to die. Oh my God! She knows now. I must play dumb

and pretend my marriage is good and better than ever. I must make her think my

husband told me to call her, even though a month has passed since she contacted him,

and her ex-husband warned me of their conversation. Now she confronts my husband

with the truth. I call her back an hour later. She doesn't care. She lets me know she

doesn't need them in her child's life.

She lets me know that Our Father, which art in heaven has met and provided all of

their needs and her son will grow up and be of great nation and an NFL player. She lets

me know she is aware of everything, and now she is successful with a degree. She

states she has learned to trust and depend on God. She is saved now, she informed me

as we talked on the phone. She was not the same woman I knew years ago, she has

changed. She is very professional now. I got to see a picture of this child, because he is

deep in my soul. He belongs to my husband. An unhidden truth will one day be

revealed. A planned, switched DNA; his looks and character will never be shielded.

"Visitation"

She came to visit me, I didn't know why; I followed her to see my surprise.

Everyone yelled, "Where are you going?" I yelled, "I'll be back," as I followed

Grandma around the corner. We sat on a couch that was in a little room, as the

surroundings looked familiar "Oh Grandma! Oh Grandma! I miss you so much." She

looked, smiled and stared with a glow that lit up the room. With a soft touch to my

face, she said, "I know" she moved aside to show me my surprise, a visitation with

Antonio; I was really surprised. I was so happy and full of joy; he jumped out at me as I

caught him with a bundle of love. "I miss you! I miss you!" I said over and over. He

said, "I know," as he kissed me on my shoulder. Then I heard the sound of a sweet

little girl, who was running around, and I stared at her. I looked at her face as hers was

on mine. She looks like me" I thought to myself. And I looked at grandma, who was

still smiling. Antonio jumped down and ran around with this little girl. They knew each

other, and I thought, "It must be the child I should have had. My visit was now over, I

fell to my knees yelling, "Please don't go." Grandma grabbed their hands as they

walked through the white smoke.

"Ungodly Soul Ties"

After running into ungodly men and being attached to ungodly soul ties, I knew I had

to make a change in my life. I was tired of settling for less; I was tired of getting

second best. I bed one night, I prayed to God, "Detached me from ungodly souls that

are tiring my spirit apart." I am more than a contour and more than just a bootie call;

my mind is deeper than looks and the figure of my body. I am above and not beneath. I

have not because I never asked God. After lying on the floor a few minutes and talking

to God, I felt a pull. My body jerked, and my soul was weak. I saw her as she came out

of me. She was a little girl. I became weary, and my soul was tired as a little fear came

upon me. I began to call on the name of Jesus as she

tried to get back in me. I called on the name of Jesus as my grandma had always taught

me. I laid on the floor as the Lord restored me, washed me with his blood, and filled

me with his spirit, creating me a clean heart and renewing the right spirit in me. I

knew at that point, I was forgiven seventy times seven, Matthew 18: 21- 2, NIV.

I knew after confessing my sins, John 1:9, NIV.

I was restored and made new over again; transgression was removed

Psalms 103:12, NIV. Detached and unleashed from ungodly soul ties.

"Tested with Tithe"

Sitting at my desk at work while being convicted by God, my eyes fill with tears as I

battle with my confession inside. Afraid to step out on faith because of my bills, not

knowing if I have enough to make ends meet and money to spare.

Saturday night the battle was still on my mind; I was still afraid without making up my

mind. A friend I hadn't seen in years walked up and shared a message, "Never under

estimate the Holy Spirit." My eyes watered up, but I didn't shed a tear, for the Holy

Spirit appeared to be so near. Lord, "I am at a party" for God still appeared to be near.

I knew that the next day I had to be in church, walking into church with a check in my

hands. I'm paying my tithe, and stepping out on faith.

"See My Change"

My spirit connected intimately with God as the enemy tried to find a way to defeat me. My ears opened up to his voice, while my eyes see pass the natural. It's a peace that passes all understanding and a calm that settles all storms. God takes metaphorical thinking and turns it into a blessing. See my change as God shifts me from one level to the next. I am secure with who I am and where God is taking my life. I know who I am when I put my trust in God's hands. See my change as God shifts me from one level to the next. I don't have to explain when the devil's plans don't stands. I don't have to explain when you said, "I will never amount to anything." Now, God made me better than what you expected. I don't have to explain why I still have my right mind after the death of two children, when I lost my mother, and then lost my father two weeks later.

See my change as God shifts me from one level to the next.

Look at God...

"Struggle to Breathe"

She tosses she turns, she struggles to breathe, nowhere to run, and no air to breathe.

Twenty-seven weeks old as Mommy fought and prayed to keep her alive.

It was a hard struggle as Mommy saw death creeping inside. Trapped in a hospital bed

and crying out to God, "Please help my little girl; the doctors have gone too far." She

can't breathe, and I'm getting weak, as the strain is heavy on my heart. It's a shame

how the doctors were tearing my family apart.

With one excuse the doctors had and not leaving it up to God.

He is almighty, as they never acknowledged or tired to understand how I felt.

They made a decision without seeking his face, and

one day they will have to pay, when they see God's face.

A'miya I named her; she was a very beautiful little girl.

One day I will see her again, when he ends this old world.

No more struggle to breathe, as God has giving her fresh air, wait on Mommy; when it's

my time I will be there.

"Behind the Fist"

He beat me, he stumped me, and he put me to sleep. Black eyes, cut lip, raped and

tormented at night, and afraid to go to sleep. Nowhere to run, nowhere to hide, wounds

cut so deep only God can heal from inside. It is hard when you feel you are all alone

with only an Antonio to keep you strong. I did not know how to get out and was scared

staying in. With comments from everyone, the same people didn't understand the

trouble I was in and did not help me to get away. It is easy to pass judgment from the

outside looking in; losing in a boxing ring and dying within.

Sent by Satan to abuse and destroy me while others laughed, but the beatings never

end. Grandma is gone, and I am all alone, waiting to hear her as I fell asleep,

and the nights seem long.

He possesses, deranged and full of heat; in hell he will burn from his head to his feet.

In hell he will meet the man who sent him to me. I have forgiven him for the things he

has done to me, for God has designed a new woman in me. Behind the fist I will never

be, for I will seek God in the next man I meet.

"Murder by Man"

He murdered him; he took him away, poor innocent soul and a Lamb of God.

Why I asked! What could this two year-old child have done?

His smile lights up the room; his spirit shines so bright. He changed my life at a young

age, some say for that bad, but I say for the good. I pressed my way to achieve my goals

in life, and in school every day; sometimes with black eyes.

He was a special little boy but murdered by man.

I say an evil man controlled by Satan. Some had a lot to say about the situation they

knew nothing about. I was scared to leave and scared to die.

Antonio was his name, my little angel, my heart, my joy, and my firstborn. Taken away

so soon and never experiencing what life had to offer. He was murder by a man name

Ahaz.

"Extraordinary Woman"

I am an Extraordinary Woman.

Who I am, is what God created. From the top of my head to the sole of my feet

I am an Extraordinary Woman.

A single mother allowing God to fight her battles while winning the war.

I am an Extraordinary Woman.

What they said, is what I'm not. Through my faith I'm saved by grace.

I am an Extraordinary Woman. Yes! I did it, and I'm not perfect. I'm still an

Extraordinary Woman.

God is with me and I am never alone.

I am an Extraordinary Woman.

What makes me an Extraordinary Woman?

I look past the mountains, and survived the storms.

I am a queen; I am the

CEO of my life and God is the owner and founder.

I'm beautiful inside and out.

I am an Extraordinary Woman!

Acknowledgments (abusive relationships)

There comes a time when the cycle of abuse has to be broken. We must come together and pull each other up instead of tearing each other down, stop belittling ourselves by fighting over men, and surrounding ourselves with positive people and positive things. *People only do what we allow them to do. You have the power to stop them.*

It doesn't matter where you come from, who your parents are or what you did in life to make ends meet. God is a good God, and he will forgive all your sins.

I know who I am; when I know who created me... A new beginning...

Acknowledgments (death of a child)

Grandma always said the death of a child is the worst pain in the world, and it is a pain

only God can heal. Many times after the death of my two children, I thought I did not

need counseling, and there were times I thought I was going to lose my mind. I'm not

putting down doctors, but this pain I was feeling was beyond what a doctor could do

and far beyond what school could teach. I had to get on my knees and contact a doctor

I knew could feel my pain. I didn't want to be on medication; I wanted to be in my

right mind, and I didn't want to sit down and explain my life story. I tried counseling

and sometimes I felt worse coming out than I did going in.

The greatest love in the world was giving birth to all my children and seeing their little

faces after they were born. For two to be taken away without explanation was the pain I

was dealing with. " I felt if you didn't experience it, you couldn't help me, "I always

said to myself. So I called on God. He lost his son Jesus for us to have a second chance

at life. My wounds are healed, and I am able to release my kids to him and the pain I

held in my heart. I know I will see them again. I teach my children now to live right,

and the will see them one day. My heart is full of joy knowing they are in my father's

hand.

We are never apart...

Building Comprehensive Solution to Domestic Violence

"You are a rose, a woman designed with her own fragrance. Wonderfully made by God"

Building Comprehensive Solution to Domestic Violence

Topic:

- Breaking the Cycle

- Healing

- Forgiveness

- Finding Your Purpose

- Loving Yourself

- New Beginnings

Did You Know?

- 1 in 3 women and 1 in 4 men have been victims of physical violence by an intimate partner within their lifetime

- Domestic victimization is correlated with a higher rate of depression and suicidal behavior

- There are more than 20,000 phone calls placed to domestic violence hotlines nationwide

- Women abused by their intimate partners are more vulnerable to contracting HIV or other STI's due to forced intercourse or prolonged exposure to stress

Week 1

"Breaking the Cycle"

Breaking the Cycle

Identifying

The

Problems

Repentance

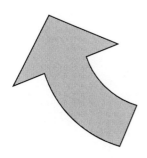

**What does it mean
to identify the
problem?**

"Our fathers have sinned, and are not; and we have borne their iniquities."
Lamentations 5:7

*"For the law of the Spirit of life in Christ Jesus hath made me free from the
law of sin and death"*
Romans 8:2

Indentifying the Problem

Identify and Define the Problem. The first step in the problem solving is to identify and define the problem. A well-defined problem often contains its own solution within it, and that solution is usually quite obvious and straightforward.

What does it mean to identify the problem?

Problems directly or indirectly related to a desired outcome or standard of behavior. Identifying a very clearly defined and specific problem is the first critical step to successfully implementing the process.

What are some problems you may have identified?

1.
2.
3.
4.
5.

Week 2

"Healing"

Healing

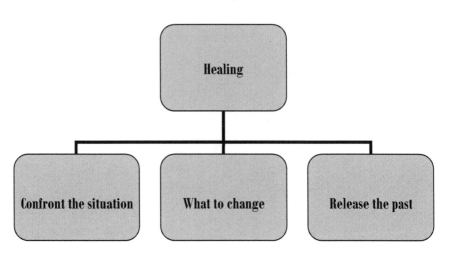

"Faith without works is useless."

James 2:20

"Heal me, O Lord, and I will be healed; save me and I will be saved, for you are the one I

praise."

Jeremiah 17:14

"So do not fear, for I am with you; do not be dismayed, for I am your God. I will

strengthen you and help you; I will uphold you with my righteous right hand."

Isaiah 41:10

Healing

Healing is a process; it requires forgiving others and yourself. It require stepping out of denial and into reality, releasing anger, not allowing yourself to feel depressed and acceptance things that happen you cannot change.

Seven steps to healing:

1. **Acceptance**

2. **Prayer**

3. **Reconstructing your life**

4. **Meditate on healing**

5. **Forgiving yourself as well as others**

6. **Faith**

7. **Trust yourself as well as the process**

Confront the situation

Accept and completely acknowledge the truth of what is happening in your life. Observing yourself and accepting responsibility, understanding the root of the problem, it is important to identity the real issues. Separate your feelings about the issue you want to talk about from other perplexing situations or emotions that aren't relevant to the discussion.

Want Change

The most important step toward personal spiritual growth is the desire to grow. Spiritual growth and development is not a goal it is a lifelong journey that requires time, energy and dedication. When the newness of your new spiritual growth wears off, you may be tempted to give up. Do give up keep pushing and trust the process.

What do want to change?
1.
2.
3.
4.
5.

Release the Past

The past is history, and there is nothing you can do to change it. Holding on to past events keeps you from experiencing new ones, and the emotional baggage will only weighs you down. Accept these past events, both good and bad, as learning experiences and move on with life.

What do you want to release?
1.
2.
3.
4.
5.

Week 3

"Forgiveness"

Forgiveness

Forgiveness doesn't excuse their behavior; it's a new beginning to healing and starting a new life.

Forgiveness is "letting go of bitterness and revenge."

Six steps to forgiveness:

1.   Acknowledge the pain

2.   Choose to forgive

3.   Not seeking revenge

4.   Ask for forgiveness

5.   Choose to be happy

6.   Let Go

Self questions:

1.   What is preventing me from forgiveness?

_____

2.   How do I forgive myself?

_____

In most situations forgiving others may be a simple, or it may be a fight. The mind can sometimes cling to our resentments, broken relationships, and unresolved conflicts. As you prepare for this new journey, remember that the Lord is always with you.

God desires that we seek forgiveness?

Psalm 32; Matthew 18:21-35

Week 4

"Finding your Purpose"

Finding your Purpose

1. Finding what drives you

2. What makes you happy and what come easy to you

3. Taking the steps to find your life purpose

4. Following what your heart is telling you

5. Deciding where you want to go

6. Be clear and honest with yourself

7. Take time for yourself

8. Setting realistic goals

Blessed are all who wait for Him

Isaiah 30:18

He is still in control and will perfect that which concerns you

Psalm 138:8

And we know that in all things God works for the good of those who love him, who have been called according to his purpose.

Roman 8:28

Week 5

"Loving Yourself"

Loving yourself

Feeling praiseworthy requires you to see yourself with fresh eyes of self-awareness and love. Acceptance and love must come from within.

1. Accepting where you are right now

2. Letting the past go

3. Practicing the kind of love you aspire to receive

4. Shift your self-perception

5. Take time to meditate; reflect on happiness

6. Work on personal and spiritual development

7. Forgive yourself

8. Focus on being positive

9. Eliminate toxic people in your life

Whoever gets sense loves his own soul; he who keeps understanding will discover good.

Proverbs 19:8

You are altogether beautiful, my love; there is no flaw in you

Solomon 4:7

Week 6
"New Beginning"

New Beginning
"Prayer"

Dear heavenly Father as I come you, I arise to establish my legal right and take back everything Satan has stolen from me. Father God I ask you to forgive me for all my sins. Delivered me Father from every generational curse going four generation back on my Mother side of the family and my Father side of the family. Father God I ask you to deliver me and break every ungodly soul ties from every sexually partner. God, I ask that you protect our minds. Father, the mind set on the flesh is death, but the mind set on the Spirit is life and peace. Romans 8:6. Let us not be conformed to this world, but be transformed by the renewing of our minds that we may prove what your will is, that which is good and acceptable and perfect. Romans 12:2. God surround me with your favor as with a shield. Psalm 5:11-12 . God strengthen me in your power, dress me in your armor so that I can stand firm against the schemes of Satan. God you know my struggles and it's not against flesh and blood, but against the rulers, against the powers, against the world forces of this darkness, against the spiritual forces of wickedness in the heavenly places. Ephesians 6:10-12 Deliver me Father and make me whole again. Show me how to rebuild my life and I can do your WILL.

Protection

Father God you said in your Word "No weapon form against me shall prosper" Isaiah 54:17, God protect me and my children. Lord, I pray physical and spiritual protection over my generation, keep evil from my family. I bind every ungodly ancestry spirits from my ancestors on both sides of my family.

I pray you will make me and my family strong in the presence of danger, recognizing that you God will overcome and will set right all injustice and wrong one day.

Blessings

Father I speak the blessings of Abraham over my life and my children lives. Father as you said in Deuteronomy 28 6-8. Open my eyes and expand my territories that I may use the opportunities to bring glory to your name as you said in your work 1 Chronicles 4:10, Guide my footsteps daily and lead me away from danger. Father I will always remain humble and willing to serve and bless others. Father I thank you for a new beginning. Father I thank you for loving me and being a blessing to me and my family. God I thank you that your love and favor has no end. In Jesus Name, Amen

---

(Your Name)

Book of Deuteronomy blessed me
Book of Proverbs prepared me
Book of Psalms protected me
Book of Nehemiah rebuild me
1 Chronicles 4:10 rebuild my faith

Made in the USA
Columbia, SC
18 June 2019